Tefl: Learn How You Can Teach English as a Foreign Language, Live Abroad & Save $12,000+ a Year!

How to teach Esl abroad, get that Efl job, find out which online Tefl course is best, get the complete lowdown on teaching English in Korea (and elsewhere in Asia) and everything you need to know about Tesl & teaching English as a Second Language

Christopher John Walker

Contents

Part I- Tefl: What You Need to Know

Part II Country Profiles

Finding Employment

Vietnam Specifics

Where to Teach

Finding Employment

Pay Rates

Work Visa

8

What This Book Can Do For _Your Life_

This book has been designed to educate, inform and to give you confidence. Too many people think about their life, about possible other lives they could have lived and be left with the question: "what if". I wonder if this book would have ever got written if I had not stumbled across a little advert on an obscure local job listings page. "Uni graduates wanted to teach English in Korea. Any discipline. No experience needed. £12,000 a year, paid accommodation and flights, 7% tax. For more details email Greg".

I had heard of teaching English as a foreign language before. Friends of mine taught in Japan after they finished their degrees, I had even take a semester of teaching English as a foreign language in my degree, but I never considered it for myself. Why not? First off I thought you needed an expensive £1,500 course (and it is very helpful but you don't need it). Then there was the question of student loans needing repaying and anyway didn't you have pay to teach English abroad?

As I wrote this book my mind traveled to the individual countries and I felt a deep longing to go to each and every one and settle there indefinitely. I truly hope this book is read by a reader who never considered teaching as a passport abroad, that it convinces another who has long put off the dream, that loans manage to get paid off quicker because of it, that people find employment and are able to contribute to society in the land of their dreams or find better jobs because of it, that it breaks the shackles of tedious, boring, mind numbing work that so many find themselves doing and shows that there is another way.

So what can TEFL do for you? It obviously depends who you are and what you want! If you're looking to live abroad either permanently or for an extended period of time then this book can help you whether you can do that without having to work fulltime, if you're going to need a steady job to support yourself or if you have very little skills and quite a lot of debt and think it'll take you a decade to be in a position to move abroad if ever. Its probable that you fall into one of these categories and may well fall into another one of them into the future.

TEFL can put a dent in your debts. Too many people are stuck in a job they hate, in a country they would love to leave but can't afford to because they have to pay of their debts first, especially college graduates. Are your loan repayments less than $1,000 a month? If not talk to someone about getting them consolidated. There are many countries where you can live a nice lifestyle AND save $1,000 a month for debts and future travel/investments/savings. If you have a bachelors degree then that is ALL you need and schools will reimburse your airfare when you get there! So you can get rid of the debts or save up a chunk of change abroad at a faster rate than you could at home!

Perpetual traveler? How about work for a year, live well, and travel the next year on the $12,000 you managed to save? Oh, and the employer will fly you in and out every year too! Or just spend the next year at your new overseas base?

Want a career that is actually fun and you can do in your dream location. TEFL can provide that! Choose between adults or children to teach. The kids are way better behaved overseas, they actually show some respect for the teacher instead of trying to stab or shoot them!

Teaching English as a foreign language is a perfect way to get out and go whether you want to do it as a means to escape only, are looking for a career, a back up employment plan or even as a revenue raising plan to help you afford that little piece of paradise! While this book will specifically focus on the Asian countries of South Korea, Japan, Taiwan and Vietnam as this is

11

where the real money in TEFL is to be made, we will also look at nearby Thailand and the general advice found in this book will be useful in helping you find and get a TEFL job in other locations.

What is TEFL?

Simply speaking TEFL is teaching English as a foreign language. Generally the student will ultimately not be able to speak and write English fluently from this alone. There are different requirements and desired outcomes depending on the learner, the organization preparing the teaching (if there is one) and the wider culture.

The desires of a student who wants to study at university in an English speaking nation will be different to that of a businessman who wants it for business meetings and different to those who see it as a social status marker. Some people want to practice conversations, some want to learn grammar and some just want a working knowledge of the language. In some schools you will be a teaching assistant, in others you will have to teach grammar. In others they get taught grammar by their regular teachers and you are there to help them with pronunciation and speaking not theoretical skills.

Apart from "TEFL" people and adverts may also use

the terms "TESOL" (Teaching of English to Speakers of Other Languages) "EFL" (English as a Foreign Language). "ESL" means "English as a Second Language" and generally means the student gets taught to a higher level than if they are being taught English as a foreign language.

Volunteer vs. Paid

Many volunteer positions exist in the world of TEFL. Often you need to pay for your own transportation to the location and you might even have to pay a fee for admin costs, food and accommodation. This isn't always the case but it often is. Sometimes the fees will not be expensive at all and sometimes they will be extremely high. Occasionally you may get room and accommodation in exchange for volunteering, but by their very non-commercial nature volunteer jobs cost you more than just your time but your cash as well.

Perhaps the best volunteer organization for TEFL teachers to be with is The Peace Corps; *http://www.peacecorps.gov/*. It initially consists of several months training followed by at least 2 years volunteer work. They will provide a locally indexed living wage and free complete medical/dental healthcare. The Peace Corps also pays for travel to and back from your destination and provides a small bonus when you leave them. American graduates can get their student loan repayments deferred while they are with the Peace Corps.

In the Asian countries it is very possible to make fairly

decent money, live a nice lifestyle and save $12,000 a year- this is a decent amount of money by western standards and more than I could save back home with a job that paid double a TEFL wage, but when you consider that you can live in luxury traveling some of the poorer Asian countries for a year on that money you understand why many lucky people work a year in Korea or Japan, travel for a year and do it all over again.

Schools vs. Private Lessons

The two main ways of making money by teaching English is either by being employed by a school or by teaching private lessons. Schools are often able to arrange a work visa for you meaning you can stay longer in the country without having to leave or go on a visa run (leaving the country and re-entering thereby renewing your "tourist" visa), they also provide some stability in regards to income coming in and many will provide accommodation for you. Most that do not will help you find accommodation that you need locally. Some although not all also offer training before you start and some even have lesson plans already set out.

Private lessons can generally make you more money, but can't provide you with things like a work visa, stable income or accommodation. In most countries teaching privately on a tourist visa is illegal and in many it's illegal to teach privately without your employer's permission. Despite this many people do so as it is fairly hard to prove you are teaching privately and private English lessons don't usually get raided! Most who teach privately start teaching with a school and pick up a few private lessons slowly to begin with and through referrals and word of mouth build up a network. Sometimes it is more profitable to then stop working with the school and just teach privately although you do then have to think about your visa situation. In an ideal world many would try and convince the sponsoring school to let them work just a day or half a day maybe even for free in return for the work visa while teaching privately the rest of the time.

Children vs. Adults

Working with children and working with adults is different but the same!

Often a child may have a higher level of English than an adult.

Generally speaking if you are working for a school then the adults you will be teaching will be enrolled for business reasons; they can earn more and be promoted quicker if they speak English, to talk to associates overseas etc.

Adults are more likely to not just want to know what is right but why it is right.

Equally though many adults just want conversation practice- they may have been taught English when they where younger but not from a native speaker so they want to make sure they can pronounce words correctly.

Short Term vs. Long Term

Teaching English is possible both short term and long. From just a one year stint in a country to check it out, or to keep traveling or teaching English if you wish. Longer term it is possible to keep teaching indefinitely in one country or in many although if you don't currently have savings you might want to think about retirement or when you are no longer able to teach.

Obviously some of the higher paying locations may enable you to save money and perhaps buy housing or start a business in a cheaper location where immigration is more lax should you choose to stop working altogether. For those who want a career out of TEFL but want to get better paid jobs then you will have to get two things: experience and qualifications.

The better paid jobs generally require a Masters degree (many Asian universities specify that this cannot be an online or distance learning degree even if it is from a reputable university). Most often any Masters is acceptable although Masters degrees in Applied Linguistics or TESOL may be slightly favored. If you wish to get a job in an English speaking country at a University teaching English as a Foreign Language you will require either the Masters in Linguistics or a Masters in TESOL.

The best teaching jobs in non English speaking countries to get if you wish to make a career out of TEFL would be in universities around the world (which often require a Masters), or in schools which would require an Education degree, Masters in Education or a teaching conversion degree (the PCGE in the UK).

Alternatively you could work your way up from within a school to be a director (hiring teachers, administrating etc) however generally those who earn the most within the TEFL profession are those who own schools which when you are a teacher yourself and have contacts could turn out to be surprisingly easy in some locations if you are business minded.

What is Required to Teach English as a Foreign Language?

Most of the information that is found once you have decided to research the possibility of teaching English abroad is either vague, misleading, contradictory, outdated or simply wrong. It is quite possible, and quite unfortunate that someone could spend a month or more looking for information on TEFL and conclude that you need a graduate degree to teach anywhere, another might be persuaded that absolutely no qualifications are necessary for any country or job, another that there is no chance of saving money unless you are "substantially frugal in some Asian countries, but even then it is unlikely" (I nearly hit the computer when I read that statement) a lucky individual might come to discover that it is indeed possible to live a comfortable life and still save $12,000 US a year and get their flights reimbursed if they have a BA and teach in South Korea. But that still wouldn't be telling the whole story.

This section will look at what is really required for you to teach English as a foreign language.

Of course it is important to remember that different countries have different minimum requirements, although these are not always enforced. For instance many kindergarten schools are happy to employ foreign teachers in Taiwan, something that is technically illegal but which many thousands of people do each year with almost no problem at all. It is up to you to ultimately decide whether something is a worthwhile risk and whether you think it is morally right to do something that is illegal even though the country's government and immigration system may not take it seriously.

First we will look at the issue of being a native speaker of English and the part of the world you come from, we will look at your grammatical ability (or lack thereof!), race issues, gender issues, qualifications and age regulations - there is a huge amount of misinformation surrounding this last issue.

Native Speaker

Many people assume that you can only teach English as a foreign language if you are a native English speaker, others assume that being able to speak the language is all you need, yet others think that ability to speak English does not qualify you to teach English as a foreign language. All are wrong! Being able to speak English is the basic qualification to teach English as a foreign language. If you are a native speaker then you have most of the tools required to TEFL. The students are attempting to learn to effectively communicate in English; no future trade partner is going to be surprised at a foreigner failing to keep the correct details of grammar to the finest point.

Bottom line, if English is your first language then they want to be able to understand you, you to understand them and for them to talk at your level- not the ability to write a thesis in the Queens English! Obviously just being a native speaker alone isn't enough... you cant expect to walk into the local square sit down and have people suddenly burst forth in English by simply being in your presence and spontaneously shower you with money! You need to know how to get a job and at least know the very basics of how to give people that knowledge. If you are a parent you already have some of this knowledge- how do you think your kids managed to learn English?

In this section we must talk about the country that

native speakers come from and their dialect. The TEFL world is broadly divided between the United States and Great Britain Most initiatives come from these two countries, overwhelmingly most teachers are from these two countries and both sets have a large number of teachers who fairly vocally think that their accent and version of English is more relevant and produces better teachers!

The truth is that if you have a classic neutral American or British accent then you are going to be in huge demand. Very occasionally some individual schools or employers will show preference to American teachers or to British teachers. This is complicated even more because schools in the same city may have different preferences.

If you have a regional accent then you might occasionally find that schools will overlook you in favor of someone with a "better" (easier to understand) accent. However if you speak clearly, and if necessarily slowly then you should be fine. A rule of thumb is that if someone from London or New York cant tell if you are speaking English or not then you might have to learn to speak more clearly and try and drop the accent slightly (just do your best impression of "those city folk"!).

Canadians, Australians, Kiwis and the Irish will all find themselves work without too much hassle either. South Africans may find it hard in some countries to get a work visa if they don't have a passport from one of the countries listed above. Many schools won't mind employing you but sometimes getting a visa may be hard and frustratingly South African's are often denied and approved visas from the same country depending on which official is handling your paperwork!

Grammatical Ability

Most graduates I know don't have a clue about grammar. This includes the English (the subject) graduates. In fact it is especially true for English graduates. I can say this as I graduated with an honors degree in English and Philosophy, having taken degree level TEFL courses at university and still not knowing the difference between a noun and an adverb. If this was true for me, how many others must it also be true for?

English is one of the most complex languages in the world grammatically speaking. There are rules, and sub rules and exceptions to rules and exceptions to the exceptions to rules! This is what makes teaching English to non-English speakers difficult once they get to an advanced level and why teachers of English as a second language need higher qualifications and skills than EFL teachers- their students are trying to master the system for speaking and the system doesn't seem to make sense. That is because the system doesn't make sense! What is true for these students is true to a lesser degree with EFL students.

You, if you are a native speaker, have an enormous

advantage though. You intuitively, without needing to analyze it know English grammar because you use it every day without thinking. You don't need to wonder why "the cat sits on the mat" is wrong if "the cat" has been dead for two years. You may however need a little help in working out the correct words to use instead: "the cat used to sit on the mat"; "I remember when the cat sat on the mat". Don't stress about grammar though! I said it was complex and it is not unusual for really bored, uptight, miserable and "better than you" teachers (there are people like this in any profession if you look hard enough) to argue for hours over whether a term is grammatically correct or not- and never find out for sure.

What the learners want is to be understood. If it sounds funny, if it sounds wrong then it needs to be corrected. If you, your family, your old boss and half your neighborhood would accept the statement and get really confused trying to work out if it was grammatically correct if asked then you generally don't need to worry!

TEFL courses and qualifications are there to teach you the basics of how to teach, and teach you what you need to know in order to teach EFL, including grammar. You will know lots of it instinctively, and it will give practical guidelines on how to teach it. If you are really worried about grammar then it is extremely important that you take a TEFL course that shows you how to teach it. Remember, teachers are allowed to look at the answer book in class!

It should also be noted that many TEFL situations wont require hardly no grammar at all (I couldn't resist that one!). Lots of schools like in Asia have you there to teach conversational English; for instance in South Korea the lesson plans are already prepared by the Korean teachers. Your students will often have been taught English in their school system but not had the chance to practice with a native speaker.

Even if you are there to teach an actual lesson most schools will give you a book which you follow and hopefully add something of your own into the lesson. When you're teaching in Asia, that is most often what you are there for, to provide a fun experience with a native English speaker.

Race

Of all the possible barriers to TEFL this is one that people either assume will be a huge obstacle or assume will have no influence at all and get extremely angry if it does. In Western democracies racism is highly illegal. It is also highly prevalent. We like to shove it under the carpet and pretend it doesn't exist. We are shocked if people from other nations make racist comments or we perceive racism but it happens all the time at home and is ignored. It would be quite wrong to suggest that race is no issue at all in the world of TEFL. It is not as big an issue as some people make it out to be. By the very nature of our culture those who have experienced racism abroad or think that they may have been denied jobs on their ethnicity will be much more likely to draw attention to the fact.

Some schools and employers would prefer a pretty or handsome white, tall, blonde tutor than someone from another ethnic group. The reasons for this could be that a person of that description is what they think clients will want, a misguided and uninformed impression that a person like that will be a better teacher or the employer may simply be racist. If you come up against this then the actual reason is more likely to be that many "locals" have in the past pretended to be Asian-American's, Asian-Brits etc in order to pick up a higher wage; white skin may be falsely seen as "protection" and a "guarantee" that the teacher is a native English speaker.

There will be people who will tell you that in Asian countries if you are not white you probably won't get a job and if you are Asian looking you can forget about it. Some schools are like this, especially if the parents see a white teacher as a status symbol, but there are many who do not. There are many non-white English teachers in Korea and beyond who have managed to get a job without trouble including a huge number of Asians which blows that concern out of the water!

It may surprise you but the majority of teachers who feel some sort of racism, however slight, are white. While it is not right, many other ethnicities have experienced racism at home however many white people have not. While it is true that many cultures will respect you because you are a teacher, Western (and even because you are white) Caucasians are a minority in Asia and so you may feel people are staring at you. They may be. They may not be used to seeing someone of your ethnicity very often. It is important to factor this in as it can be quite disconcerting. This is not something that is unique to TEFL, it is something that needs to be considered by whoever wishes to live in a foreign land among a largely different race when you are used to being the majority and the establishment.

Gender Issues

Like race, gender hiring issues generally aren't a problem. There are generally more female teachers than male.

Some cultures show a slight favor to females applying for kindergarten age jobs over males (as exists in our own culture arguably).

Individual schools may hire someone for their looks in the application photo over any real reason but there are just as many companies in the western world who hire someone because the interviewer finds them attractive. It may happen.

It won't stop you getting a job soon if you miss out on that particular one because of it, and if you get the job because of your looks… well, as in any job, make it clear they hired an employee and not a girlfriend!

Age

The issue of the age of the potential TEFL is one that rises again and again. It makes me fairly angry actually! I have heard again and again the question asked "I'm X years old… am I too old… TEFL is a young person's game isn't it?" No! It is not a "young person's game". True the young adapt very well to TEFL, and the entry level wages are often lower than a middle aged, professional, college educated person may be able to earn at home but you are not too old (unless you are on your hospital bed and the priest is reading this to you because he forgot to bring the last rites sheet with him). I have heard people ask if they are too old at 26!

The reason lots of people think they are too old is that most of the marketing of TEFL is aimed at gap year students. Most TEFL teachers are older, often a lot older. They tend to fall into two broad categories of 26-32 and 40+. This is a huge generalization and you will find a large number of teachers of every age including 60+. Most people taking TEFL certification courses within the US, UK and Canada are 30+ and many are retired.

Some schools prefer older teachers, some younger. Age

is not however a barrier to getting a teaching job in any country. Period. Schools often like the idea of an older teacher as in many cultures elder people are equated with wisdom. But being young isn't going to affect employment either. Your main skill is that you speak English and can look reasonably presentable. Don't be worried about factors like age!

As far as marketing to gap year students is concerned there is a very good reason. Most schools that teach English as a foreign language are on the other side of the world. They make a profit but are not huge (outside the big chains, which do often prefer youngsters because they feel they can pay them less and will do exactly as they are told), they can get teachers without advertising the industry and don't feel that they need to reach millions of potential new teachers to fill the 10 positions they have a year, they tend to see advertising a job on an internet job board as a huge marketing campaign they may not have the resources or knowledge to pull off. Unless they also teach CELTA or a similar course for would be English teachers then there is no real need to advertise.

The big players money wise in the TEFL industry are not really the certification providers (CELTA the industry standard is produced by the world famous Cambridge University, although individual schools who teach the classes often advertise) but by companies offering gap year TEFL courses. They have access to a huge market (17 and 18 year olds about to start university), who want to see the world, have an adventure, do some good, don't expect to get paid a salary yet, are willing to rough it and have parents who are willing to pay- especially if there is a big home based company they can yell at if anything does go wrong!

These kids are trained overseas in a TEFL course, then stay with a local family, get pocket money and have their parents pay up to $10,000 or more for the privilege! That works out at a tidy profit per applicant. No wonder the gap year firms advertise so heavily and get themselves into the press more than anyone else. I don't blame them, it makes good business sense and I think it makes the kids who take the course grow a lot too. It's just that there is no reason for these companies tell people that a graduate can get free flights to Korea, a rent free apartment, only pay 5% tax, live a very comfortable life and save $12,000 in the year they are there. A graduate isn't going to get his parents to pay the companies $10,000 for telling him or her this!

Qualifications

This is dependent on where you teach and the institution within it. We'll look at some the main TEFL qualifications and then look at degrees which are required by lots of country's immigration departments as well what to do if you don't have one.

CELTA

CELTA is the "Certificate in English Language Teaching to Adults". It is now undeniably the most widely recognized teaching qualification internationally and equally enables you to get a job teaching children although it is geared toward adult learning. While it is possible to get a decent job without a CELTA it is highly recommended.

It is administrated by Cambridge University and is an intensive 4 week course which can also be done part time. Apart from the name value of the qualification which shows you know what you are doing you will also receive at least 6 hours supervised teaching with genuine English language students at least two different levels. This experience before going into a classroom is as invaluable as being able to write lesson plans from scratch which you will also learn to do. As the course is standardized future employers will know exactly what level your teaching is and what to expect from you. This also means that you can take the CELTA course anywhere in the world without worrying what quality the instruction you receive will be.

It is worth considering doing the CELTA course in the country you wish to teach in. Many local course providers are able to find their students jobs on completion, give you contacts there and finding a job once you are in the country is infinitely easier than finding one from abroad no matter what the country. The schools, even if they are unable to guarantee you a job, are in a much better position to suggest schools you can teach in, locations that may need teachers, where former students taught etc. The CELTA website with the list of accredited course providers has been included. CELTA courses generally cost about £1,500 no matter where they are taken worldwide.
The official CELTA website can be found at: *http://www.cambridgeesol.org/teaching/celta.htm* and you can find officially accredited schools worldwide at *http://cambridgeesol-centres.org/centres/teaching/index.do*

CertTESOL

Administrated through Trinity College London, this has traditionally been viewed as being roughly equivalent by employers around the world and like the CELTA can be studied in different places around the world.

It contains widely the same content as a CELTA course but in my opinion CELTA has now overtaken it as the qualification most worth having. CELTA is getting a wider acceptance among Americans than the CertTESOL and this combined with the already high popularity in the Commonwealth countries means that CELTA is likely to continue to have a wider appeal.

This in no way diminishes the usefulness of a CertTESOL in most employers' eyes. In the choice between a CertTESOL and any other TEFL certificate (other than CELTA) the CertTESOL will undeniably open more doors, and is of equal value in terms of preparing you to teach.

It also costs £1,500.

Trinity's webpage for the CertTESOL is *http://www.trinitycollege.co.uk/* and you can access their list of course providers worldwide from *http://www.trinitycollege.co.uk/locator/course_flash.ph p*

MA TESOL

Still the most favored qualification for American EFL teachers. If you eventually want to work as an EFL teacher in a University in the States or another English speaking country then you need this type of qualification.

It has serious downsides though; the price is hugely expensive and it tends very theoretical as opposed to the hands on and relevance of the CELTA or CertTESOL certificates although some MA TESOL courses do have a practical part now. For practical teaching experience CELTA in particular is becoming more and more accepted in the US.

However, having any masters degree it will enable you to get better jobs in Universities in Asia.

This does make it a somewhat attractive option, but the price is a big issue. I have heard of some universities on the East coast of the US charging $50,000 for a MA TESOL, and if you are a UK "home student" it will cost about £4,000 in fees alone.

Other Courses

There are many, many other courses available designed to teach you to teach English as a foreign language, some are good, some are ok and some are bad. The main problem with this isn't that you need to do some checking to see if a course is good or not, but that the school that employs you won't know.

If it is a case of doing a cheaper course or no course then by all means take the cheaper course. There may even be some moderately good online courses but I cannot recommend them over CELTA or CertTESOL, for one thing it is impossible to get any real teaching experience in an online environment.

The one possible exception to this is English International *http://www.english-international.com/*. It's run by a CELTA instructor and contains a video observation element. I know of a number of language school directors who are willing to hire teachers on the strength of the video observation element of the course who would never normally employ teachers with an online TEFL qualification.

If you really can't afford to do a CELTA or CertTESOL now and I had to give advice about finding a cheap online course then it would be to look for something that will teach you methodology. That is how to structure a lesson, activities and games that improve your lesson and make it more enjoyable while actually teaching the students something at the same time.

Another possible option is i-i. The advantage of this online course is that at least they have a program and network of schools worldwide to place you with once you take the course. It may also be worthwhile for those who want a cheaper course and the added guarantee of work when they first go to a country. It's a 40-hour online course: *http://www.onlinetefl.com/*

Bachelors Degree

This is dependant on where you teach and the institution within it. It has generally been accepted in the industry that to get a job in a country that pays well you need a bachelors degree. This is not necessarily true, but without help from people in the know it may as well be. Korea and Japan are widely regarded as the best places for new teachers to go as all that is needed is a degree (and that is only because the government demands it, most schools wouldn't mind) and nothing else. The lessons are planned by the Korean teachers, and it is often the same in Japan too. Other places that pay well generally require a degree and a TEFL certification and/or experience. It is more than possible to find employment with just TEFL qualification, and in some places just through being a native speaker. It is possible to get work in Japan without a degree but you do need three years experience.

The basic rule here is more is always better. If you have no teaching experience and a degree then you may well be allowed to teach in Korea but surely it is better to take at least a cheap $400 internet TEFL course than nothing else to set you in good stead if you can afford it. And if you can possibly afford it why not take the universal recognized CELTA course? True it costs about £1,500 but it opens up a lot of doors as it shows you have been trained by a professional body. It will also mean that you will be able to teach, manage the classroom and even instruct grammar competently! It also only takes four weeks to complete, but is of University level difficulty. That said if you can't afford a TEFL course I suggest teaching in Korea or possibly Japan to get a basis and then either take a course with money saved or use the experience you've gained to continue teaching in countries where you don't need qualifications. Remember though schools won't turn you away if you are TEFL qualified but they might if you are not!

Going back to the degree for a while (if you don't have one don't skip this section!), lots of countries visa regulations will not allow you a visa to teach without one and require you to bring your certificate/transcriptions with you or send them to the school to confirm you hold them. Associated degrees are not good enough nor are diplomas. When it is just the school who wants degree holders it is not uncommon for applicants just to lie and most schools do not bother checking up. When it is a foreign government asking though you cannot just lie because they want to see some proof.

Ask any "expert" in the TEFL profession or post in any TEFL discussion forum on the internet that you want to teach in a place like South Korea, Japan without a degree or with an Associate Degree and a TEFL certificate and they will not only tell you that it cant be done but will quite likely get very angry at you if you push the question. This is because so many people who are not degree educated would love the chance to take jobs here and experience a lifestyle and save more money than they would be able to back home, and the experienced EFL teacher gets fed up of explaining that they can't do it. If you are in the middle of a degree or can get one I would recommend it wholeheartedly. If however you do not and cannot for whatever reason then there is a way. I would ask that if you choose to take this path that you don't tell anyone or widely advertise it as it will only rock the boat for others and the loophole may be closed.

Some of you may already be thinking along the right lines. A few years ago "diploma mills" hit the headlines. These are basically fake degrees/transcripts that were not accredited by anyone. If you are really desperate you could buy these but I wouldn't recommend it. They are fake universities where you can buy a degree. The problem is they have a nasty habit of not following through on promises, being illegal, and occasionally getting shut down.

It is probably worth pointing out about an investigation way back in 2004. CBS did an investigative report and found out that many senior government officials had "fake degrees" from institutions that didn't exist; including the Assistant Secretary of Defense, and employees at the Transportation Security Administration, the Defense Intelligence Agency and the Departments of Treasury and Education. If they are good enough to fool those employing for the US government they may just be good enough to get a visa for TEFL work!

A better, new alternative are the "life experience" degrees. These are a very close cousin of the diploma mill "fake degrees" except they found a loophole. The big plus to this is that their offices are not going to get raided and put out of business, this means that if the school or government contacts them for verification that you hold a degree with them they will be able to confirm that. They are accredited but not by a body that the US Department of Education recognizes (it didn't stop the DoE hiring employees on the strength of those non-DoE accredited degrees though!). As long as you aren't using them to continue into further education then you will be fine.

The loophole used is the same basis that regular universities can offer honorary degrees- basically on life experience. For under $500 you can get a bachelors degree. You generally need 4 years work or "life experience" in any field. This amount of time can be reduced if you have college credits. "Life experience" includes previous job experience, military training, previous educational achievements, volunteer or community service events, and even homemaking experience, "personal goals, lifestyle, hobbies and traveling… Independent reading, viewing, listening or writing"! Many services offer free evaluation and as some point out the fact they are legal degrees is not technically based on "life experience" but on "learning, regardless of how it was obtained".

The companies listed below are all registered for distance learning and you are thus allowed to list them in your job applications and even your passport (Dr if you became a PhD- the medical field is the exception they will not issue medical degrees). The degrees are fully verifiable and there is usually a small admin fee attached when a potential future employer or government agency checks to verify. The physical Certificates are all university quality parchment and you will also get a copy of transcripts etc. Make sure that the transcripts are not just marked "pass" or "fail" as many of the diploma mill degrees were. Most life experience degrees should give a percentage mark or distinctions, high distinctions etc but check to make sure. One of these colleges (Concordia) is even accredited by a foreign state which makes it a legal accredited degree.

This is however a "grey area". Many schools will not care especially if you have a CELTA or CertTESOL qualification. Many might, especially if the person doing the hiring is an old school academic, they may well see it as cheating the system. I personally do have a four year bachelors degree, but if I didn't and was looking to get into TEFL I would probably get one of these "life experience" degrees. This is a highly important topic that I have not seen discussed openly at all other than to immediately dismiss it. Teachers think that a crackdown on teachers with "false credentials" include life experience degrees, but in reality whenever there is a crackdown it is due to fake (as in forged) degrees from traditional Universities. Consequently most of the TEFL world thinks that there is no way round the degree rule apart from a bribe and any mention of these degrees is highly taboo. Let's keep it that way! A few are listed below but if you want to find more then Google is your friend!

Almeda University *http://almedauniversity.org/*
Belford University *http://www.belforduniversity.org/*
Breyer State University *http://www.breyerstate.com*
Concordia College and University
http://www.concordia-college.net
Suffield University *http://www.suffielduniversity.com*

Finding a Job

Later in the book we will look more specifically at different regions and the countries within. Some countries have a TEFL industry that makes advice plentiful and direct, and warnings can be made with confidence. Other countries have less of an infrastructure with regards to TEFL let alone a uniform one-size-fits-all industry. What this book does endeavor to do is to give you the best possible guide on how to get a job in each of these regions and countries, what your chances of getting work are, the rough pay scale you should hold out for and resources to help you find a job.

There are general tools and processes that you can use to find a job anywhere and we will look where it is relevant about specific regions. Often though this is impractical; how much will it cost to rent a place in Japan for instance? It depends where in the country, what region, the area in the town or city, how many rooms and a whole host of variables.

The general tools will help you and there may be specific advice but always remember to research yourself too. A guide book to the specific region you want to move to, searching on the internet for specifics related to where you want to go. Transport links, weather, rent prices, entertainment all these are very specific and can change over a fairly short period of time in some instances.

There is Some General Advice Though:

Jobs will often be advertised in the following ways:

Online either directly by the school or by an agency. This is always the easiest, most cost effective way of finding employment. It is of course a risk both for you and your employer as you haven't seen the school, your accommodation or your boss and they haven't seen you- either as a teacher or as a person. They will usually be willing to help with securing a visa if they have advertised on the web though. When applying for internet postings there are a couple of things to remember:

If it looks too good to be true then it probably is. Not always but most probably. How can a school afford to pay 2 or 3 times the amount everyone else in that area/country can? If it is a government program or a more prestigious school they might, but more pay usually means you need more experience and/or qualifications.

Never get hurried into signing a contract, especially if the recruiter says there are only one or two places left. It would be better to miss out on a job than to get rushed into accepting and finding out you made a mistake.

Always ask to speak to current and ex teachers-preferably by email, if you just speak to current teachers then they may be in school when you talk to them and feel they can't be totally honest. Ex-teachers are always best to speak to as they will be able to give you an honest assessment. Ask them about accommodation, rates of pay, whether the pay was on time, the attitude of your boss, overtime, class sizes, if anything is expected of you "over and above" what you may think (lesson preparation time, outings, parents evenings etc), if they give any training beforehand, what level your teaching needs to be and anything else you can think of!

It's a good idea to ask the school for a one week orientation where you can observe classes and teachers. Even if they negotiate you down a couple of days is better than nothing. This lets you see how the students respond to different styles of teaching and cultural differences.

Ask the school to show you pictures of you accommodation and the area around it. Double check how far away from the school it is, and what the transport costs will be.

Will you be required to work split shifts? What kind of shifts will you have to work? If you are working for a business that trains its own staff English (or for a school who has a contract to do this) then it will probably be business hours. Kindergarten will often be mornings and school age and adults often afternoons and evenings. How many hours teaching will be required? Don't take anything that regularly has you teaching 25+ hours, fewer than 20 is best. How much preparation is needed for each class and how much other non-teaching time will you be expected to do? Does the school offer medical insurance, paid holiday time and bonuses? Does the school provide housing or if not subsidize it or help you to find suitable housing and provide a national of that country to help you sign the paperwork and make sure you get a good deal?

What textbooks does the school use? You want to make sure that they do use textbooks or else you will most likely be expected to make up the whole curriculum yourself which you shouldn't have to be doing every lesson! Do they have actives like cards, games and handouts that can be photocopied?

Ask all of this before you sign a contract but not in your initial email! Apply for the job first and if they are interested in you then you'll usually get a phone interview. After they accept you then start asking the questions. If at all possible ask for a copy of the contract in both English and the official language of whatever country the school is in. Usually the English contract means nothing and the contract in the official language of that nation means everything. If possible get a native speaker to check they say the same thing and if there are any extra details that have been added or certain points have been left out. It may be difficult to find a bi-lingual speaker but an advert in a local paper or on an internet message forum might yield results.

If they have a webpage then they may choose to advertise on this. Mostly it will just be the big schools that have a web presence. Nevertheless if you type the area you want to teach in along with something like "learn English" or "English lessons" into a search engine like ***http://www.google.com*** or look at the local yellow pages on the internet then this might throw something up. Even if they don't say that they have vacancies there will usually be an email address that you could use to ask the director if they would be interested in hiring you now or in the foreseeable future. Do consider though that schools in some countries get emails all the time from people interested in coming that never actually turn up so they might just ignore the emails!

Some schools will advertise for teachers locally. This tends to be in English language newspapers or magazines, on notice boards in popular backpacking hostels, universities or colleges.

Most schools don't advertise at all and you will need to be proactive and contact them. This is especially important if you want to teach somewhere out of the way or in a small school. Finding the schools is a lot easier when you are in the country as you can look in their paper version of the yellow pages (which is normally a lot better than the online versions), ask at bookstores that stock EFL textbooks and materials or even beat the streets and go to the schools in person and ask to see the director, if they like the look of you they might ask you to teach a sample lesson or hire you on the spot even if they wouldn't have had you phoned! Once you've found one school then even if they aren't hiring you can ask them how you can find out where the others are.

When going to schools in person it is worth phoning ahead of time and asking if you can drop in and speak to the director. It usually doesn't matter if you don't speak the local language as someone there should speak passable English- if no-one at an "English language school" speaks English you should take this as a hint that they may not be that successful, alternatively maybe you should just turn up in person anyway because they are obviously in need of your skills and may pay you accordingly!

When you turn up always look professional and smart. Avoid carrying a backpack, it would be much better for you to carry a cheap suitcase when you are job hunting. Also try to show some enthusiasm, as they are hardly likely to hire a teacher who looks bored to death at the interview. Bring copies of your CV, letters of reference and any certificates and transcripts you brought with you. It's a good idea to store these in a water-proof, damage-proof case or tube. You may also want to copy your CV onto a data stick or CD so that you can print them off at an internet café when you arrive in the country. Be warned that some schools may test your grammar or ask you to teach a sample lesson, while other schools may have a quick five minute chat and offer you a job on the spot.

CVs and Résumés

Whether you are sending CVs in response to job adverts, emailing them to schools in the hope of finding work, posting them on "work wanted" job boards like Dave's café *http://www.eslcafe.com* or taking them by hand to prospective employers there are some important things to note.

Covering letter- if you are sending them by post, email or fax you should include a covering letter. Keep it to the point, fairly short but try to convey enthusiasm about the particular school. It may be best to tell them about the time zone difference if there is one. Tell them what times they can call you in their time zone if they wish, although many schools will initially email you first. You can find out the time differences all around the world by visiting *http://www.timeanddate.com/*

Photo- Many schools will require a photo when you send them a CV. This shouldn't be a full "action pose" of you strumming a guitar like a rock god or hanging out of your car like some photo's I have seen. The attributes you are trying to convey are professionalism and enthusiasm. These should be passport style photos and make sure you dress smartly for them. Guys wear a shirt and tie, maybe a jacket and if you have long hair tie it back. Ladies, dress "office smart" not "nice" or "pretty" but it may be a good idea to wear makeup for the photo even if you usually don't. Remember to smile, and if the photo doesn't look right or looks unflattering then get it re-taken, it will be worth it.

Try to keep CV's to one page if at all possible. You need to have your name and contact information at the top of the page. This may sound obvious but make sure that they can contact you with the details you have given! If you are in the country and don't have a mobile/cell phone yet then buy one before you give schools your CV with just an email or worse a mailing address or a phone number that is from back home on it.

Make everything as easy as possible for a school to contact you because if it's too much trouble they may just go onto the next person. If you are not in the country you are applying to then remember to put your country at the end of your address on the CV. Don't assume that Texas, Kent or Northern Territory will be enough to get the mail to the United States, England and Australia respectively.

Also, if you are not in the same country that the school is in then it is best to put the country code before your phone number. Don't use a "+" but "00" as some phones won't have a "+" sign on them. You can find out what your country's international code is by visiting *http://www.countrycallingcodes.com/*

Date of birth and nationality come next. It is worthwhile to put your nationality on as if a school doesn't employ teachers of a certain nationality due to work visa restrictions then it is better to find out from the start as they will also probably not be willing to hire you illegally or fight for a work visa for you even if they really like you.

Then put down qualifications. Any TEFL or TEFL related qualifications should come first, then university/college qualifications and then high school or equivalent. Remember that the education system of your country will not necessarily be universally known and appreciated. Everyone knows what a degree is. However how many people don't know that a four year degree in America is the equivalent of a three year degree from for example the UK or Australia?

How many Americans realize that many countries hardly even recognize an Associate degree as a valid qualification let alone a degree? Many schools will have a basic knowledge but don't expect them to. Put the year and age you were when you gained each qualification. By all means put your school grades and GPA but don't expect it to mean as much as in your home country.

After qualifications put down the relevant work experience, paid or unpaid. Most language schools are not interested whether you have gaps in your employment history- 95% of their foreign teachers past and present have had gaps in their employment history! The idea isn't to list all the jobs you have had since you were 14 and all the responsibilities you have ever had. The school wants to see why they should hire you.

This means getting any relevance out of your past employment. Be creative if you've never had TEFL or teaching experience before (if you have then that should come at the top of the list). Have you ever shown anyone at work how to use a computer program? If so you have "computer software tutoring experience"! Have you read books to your kids or brothers and sisters? You have "voluntary childcare and literacy tutor/assistant experience".

This isn't dishonesty as your main skill is that you speak English, it is rather painting yourself in the best possible light and differentiating yourself from others. It should also give you confidence that you are much more talented and have far more skills than you realized. Any "tutoring", experience with children or adults and any business experience should be highlighted. Often schools who teach adults will have business clients and they often prefer someone with a business background and a background in the same industry would be even better (some schools put on classes for certain companies).

Next put down any personal qualities that you feel to be relevant. Leave out hobbies and interests unless they are directly relevant to the school or the students you want to teach. Also leave out the personal statement. Most jobs will be for a year although you may well be able to extend the contract but they're not that interested what you plan to do next and frankly don't care much about your three step plan for career progression or where you see yourself in the next five years.

I wouldn't put references on your CV but instead a line at the bottom that says "References and more information available on request". If you feel that it would be helpful to add the references at the bottom and although I personally would not as it cuts down on space, feel free to do so. If I was in the country I wanted to teach and was enquiring at a school I would bring written references. For this reason, even if you plan on getting a job before you go, I would obtain written references from between 2-4 people. These can include former employers or if necessary "upstanding members of the community" like a doctor, pastor, teacher or magistrate.

I would ask them to write a general "To whom it may concern" letter of recommendation that includes a mailing address, phone number and email address for them. Ask them to leave it undated so you can photocopy it and use it again in the future or re-use the original. This enables schools to see that you have letters of recommendation in the event that they don't actually want to physically check up on you, but also provides them an opportunity to do so if they wish to.

Accommodation

If you apply via the internet then many schools are willing to either provide you with free or discounted accommodation or to put you up temporarily and help you find accommodation locally. However if you travel to the country that you are looking for work in first then you need accommodation from the first day. After you find a job at a local language school they may well be able to help you find accommodation locally but in the meantime you will need somewhere to stay and also an idea of how much it will cost.

As much as I personally don't like them, I would have to recommend "youth" or backpacker hostels; either that or cheap guesthouses. Even if you plan on renting somewhere very soon after arriving, those first few days will most likely have to be spent in places like that. Again you can find out the addresses and prices of the hostels or guesthouses by typing the name of the place you want to go along with "hostel", "guest house", "cheap hotel" or something like that into a search engine.

A good tool to use to get an idea of how much more permanent accommodation will cost to rent is *http://www.craigslist.org/about/sites.* You could even use it to find accommodation to rent although it may be a little difficult to complete the required paperwork from outside the country. When you come to a country without a job it is always important to remember to bring more than enough cash to cover your expenses as well as deposits for rent if you will need it.

Private Lessons

Remember that if a school is sponsoring you for a visa, giving you accommodation free and maybe even paying for your flight then they will be very angry if you turn round and work for another school- don't do it, word will almost certainly get out and is the number two reason why teachers get deported for working illegally. They may not mind you teaching privately as long as your standards aren't slipping while you're working for them and aren't stealing their students from them.

Personally I still wouldn't tell them but many turn a blind eye especially if you get a couple of you private students to join up with the school from time to time. The possible exception to this is in some of the classes that are of a very big size 30+ where the students may have limited time to talk and practice, if asked it may be a good idea to take private conversational lessons with some of these types of students if they are adults (don't trust children to keep quiet to the other teachers or the director!).

You can generally charge more per hour for private lessons than you would get paid at a school- but it is wise to ask around how much the going rate for lessons is. Ask teachers, even teachers at other schools to see how much other people are charging and if they advertise in the local press or on flyers. Prices change all the time from town to town in many countries; you don't want to overcharge and get no clients nor undercharge and loose money.

Things to remember about private lessons are that it's always good to try and arrange lessons that are all in a close location if you are not having people come to you. So if you have to go to your clients then try not to accept lessons that mean you will constantly be traveling, but try and keep as many as you can concentrated location wise. If you have to choose between teaching a kid or an adult privately I would go for kids every time. They are a lot less likely to cancel because their parents make them go whereas adults are more likely to cancel lessons and stop them altogether after a few months unless they are very motivated.

The size of your lessons can be one on one, one or two/three or a group up to eight or nine at the most, with prices per person going down somewhat as the group increases. Individual prices depended on the country, size and competition locally. As the number of private clients go up you may start to get too many, you can cut the numbers by increasing prices until you have the right balance.

If teaching privately is legal or ignored by immigration

then you can advertise lessons in local newspapers and on notices and flyers put on notice boards, in corner shops, supermarkets, colleges, hospitals, places students or professional people go and medical schools. Make a list of people who may need to use English in the future and are easily able to pay for lessons (businesses, professional people) and contact them- don't just send a notice but a letter outlining your services and prices- I would get this written in the local language and proof read by someone bi-lingual and maybe explain you have had it translated for you and the level of the local language you speak- just so they aren't surprised.

A good resource to read to learn how to maximize both private lesson and school paid income is "Love Tefl Hate the Pay" *http://www.loveteflhatethepay.com*. It's not a lengthy book, more a short report, but it's recommendations are pure gold!

I would suggest charging for at least two weeks lessons in advance as this motivates clients to come to lessons and cuts drop out rate. Allow maybe two misses out of ten lessons and refund them with free lessons. Give them a receipt for lessons and if anything try and go over time rather than stop immediately on time. If you need to go beyond conversation practice and teach out of textbooks then good books to use with them are "TOEFL and Cambridge preparation" books.

Different clients will also want different things out of

the lessons. Do they want speaking practice so you just need to have a conversation, grammar lessons, pronunciation tips, beginner, intermediate, advanced? Remember that you will have to plan the lessons and provide any materials like textbooks for private lessons- so it may well be best to have taken a TEFL course and have had some teaching practice in a school before taking private lessons.

Private lessons can be almost as lucrative as your main job. I know one teacher in South Korea who was on a 2,000,000 Won ($2,000) a month contract working 4-8pm Monday-Friday. Each weekday afternoon he would do 2 hours of private tuition at 50,000 Won ($53) an hour which doubled his wage by giving him an additional $2,000 a month. 2 hours private lessons a day are neither hard to find nor unduly taxing if you have a reasonable work schedule and his rate was not untypical, in fact the last I heard he was about to raise it to 100 Won an hour.

Oh, and the number one reason why English teachers get deported for working illegally? It's the same as in every country and every other profession- they tell their partner about it and when they break up the ex-partner tells immigration along with enough information to make it easy and worthwhile enough for immigration to catch them!

General Internet Resources

Dave's ESL café *http://www.eslcafe.com/* is widely regarded as the best TEFL resource on the entire World Wide Web. There is a job board that many people advertise on because it has such a large number of potential teachers. Use common sense when applying for jobs and you will be fine. Don't assume just because they advertise on this website that the owners have checked them out because they haven't.

Their forums are also especially good. If there is a specific detail that you need to know about a region then there is often someone who can help you. A word of warning though, some of the posters can be quite negative, condescending and some of their advice may be unhelpful. Don't let that put you off though as there is some generally good advice to be found if you ask for it. The one golden rule about the forum is if you ask how something can be done and it is even slightly difficult then you'll get 5 people tell you it can't be done. Try to find the one or two who say it can be done as they will be the most helpful in showing you how.

The major TEFL job boards are
Dave's efl café *http://www.eslcafe.com/joblist/*

Esl base *http://www.eslbase.com/jobs/*
English school watch
http://www.englishschoolwatch.org/job.php
Esl pages *http://www.eslpages.com/*
Tefl.com *http://www.tefl.com/jobs/search.html*
Tefl.net *http://www.tefl.net/esl-jobs/*
The English job maze
http://www.englishjobmaze.com/

Try to find English language schools in the country's
yellow pages if it has one. The global yellow page site
can be found at
http://www.yellow.com/international.html

Some TEFL recruiters and major chains worth checking
out are below. Many have offices around the world and
may be willing to help to point you in the right
direction for their locality if they aren't able to help
you. The British Council is especially useful in this
regard although it does depend on which office you
contact! They have offices in most countries and often
in most of the big cities in lots of countries.
ACC: *http://www.acc-english.co.jp/employment/index_e.html*
AEON: *http://www.aeonet.com/aeon_index.php*
BCM: *http://www.bcm.co.kr/Group/e_recruit.htm*
Bridge-Linguatec:
http://www.bridgelinguatec.com/jobs.htm
Bell International: *http://www.bell-centres.com/jobs/list.asp*
British Council:

http://www.britishcouncil.org/teacherrecruitment.htm
Berlitz: *http://www.careers.berlitz.com*
CEC Network: *http://www.teachingoverseas.ca/*
English First:
http://www.englishfirst.com/teacherinfo/default.asp
Footprints Recruiting:
http://www.footprintsrecruiting.com/
GEOS: *http://www.geoscareer.com/*
Harmon Hall: *http://www.harmonhall.com/*
Hess Educational Organization:
http://www.hess.com.tw/careers
Interac: *http://www.interac.co.jp/recruit/cgi-bin/index.cgi/welcome/home.html*
International House:
http://www.ihworld.com/recruitment/teacher_vacanci es.asp
Inlingua:
http://www.inlingua.com/English/Jobs/main.asp
Media Kids: *http://www.mediakidsedu.com/*
Peppy Kids Club: *http://www.peppy-kids.com/pkc.html*
Shenker Institute: *http://www.shenker.com/job.php*
Tronwell: *http://www.tronwell.cl/jobs.php*
Vaughn Systems: *http://www.vausys.com/*
Wall Street:
http://www.wallstreetinstitute.com/ENGLISH/Current Vacancies.htm
Westgate: *http://www.westgate.co.jp/*
YBM Education: *http://www.ybmecc.co.kr/*

Grey & Black Lists

There are unofficial black lists (schools to avoid) and grey lists (they may or may not be dodgy) on the internet. There is nowhere that rates every single school as that would be an impossible job.

I would advise using a search engine like *http://www.google.com* and using the words "TEFL" or "ESL" or "English" or "teach" along with the name or alternatively the address of the school you are thinking of working for along with the word "blacklist" or "black list" or "greylist" or "grey list" and see if anything comes up.

Money

Any references to "$" refer to United States dollars. "£" are Great British Pounds/Pound Sterling. Other currency references that you may be unfamiliar with are the national currency of that country. You can use a currency converter to work out what the current exchange rate is as currency rates are always changing. I tend to use *http://www.xe.com/ucc/*

Always make sure you bring money with you. Even if you have a job waiting for you remember that you probably won't get paid for at least a month. How much you need depends on the country, I would always recommend taking at least $1,000 even if you have accommodation provided.

Transferring Money Home

What is the easiest way to transfer money to banks back home? Most people transfer money from the bank account they get paid into their main bank account at home. This money can go through three banks and each will a cut which will often cost you $50 or more per transaction. Of course you can cut down the amount you pay in charges by letting the money build up in you account.

There are better ways though. The best way if you have trusted friends or relatives in your home country is to get an ATM card with an Asian bank that you can use overseas. You can then send the card to your relatives and they can withdraw the money and deposit it in your home bank account. You will usually have to request this at your bank and they will have to make some changes on their computer system and maybe swipe the card. If asked why you need this facility you can try one of two responses. The first is that you will be traveling to nearby countries for a few days vacation every couple of months and may even be going home for a week soon and will need access to funds. The second option is to tell the bank employee that you will be sending the card to your elderly parents so you can support them, in most of family orientated Asia they will feel obliged to help if they can.

If for whatever reason the bank can't or won't give you an ATM card you can use overseas and you can't find a bank that can help you then the next best way of withdrawing funds is to buy a money order and send it to your bank back home. Some banks in Asia will require you apply for it and ask you to come back the next day, but it's still worth the haste. There will be an associated charge but it should be less than the cost to just transfer the money back home.

When You First Arrive

Be aware that after the first 4-6 months you will probably want to leave and go home. This is culture shock and it is perfectly normal, if you stick it out then it will get better.

If you don't have accommodation provided then you will probably have found accommodation in a tourist/ex-pat area of town. Things are likely to be louder, more expensive and often more depressing in these areas. Move out of the tourist area, start using local shops and learning the language and you'll start to notice that prices drop and people become friendlier.

Often the locals who interact with foreigners are pushy about money and are only interested in what they can get out of you. That's because it is their job! If you get out of the tourist/backpacker areas then you will meet locals who aren't dependent on selling you something for their family to survive. Instead you'll meet locals who are friendlier and may even go on to become friends.

Imagine if someone came to your home town who didn't speak English and the only people they really tried to speak to were sales assistants and charity fundraisers. They would think that the people where you live were unfriendly and only interested in extracting money from them. Even if they did meet you they wouldn't be able to communicate so why would you treat them as anything other than a foreigner? You most likely wouldn't become friends with them. That's why it's important to start to learn the language and speak to the locals. That's when everything changes.

Countries

Japan and South Korea are thought as the big two in the TEFL world with Taiwan coming a close third. A fairly new development is the emergence of Vietnam as an increasingly attractive location to the extent that some teachers may be able to save as much money in Vietnam as any of the big 3 and arguably a better standard of living.

This still hasn't been picked up on by most people in the TEFL world and will probably take at least five years before they start talking about it as being on par with the others. At the moment 3 things are stopping that: schools in Vietnam are steadfastly refusing to advertise on the web in any major way, the half decent schools all require a Celta level Tefl certificate not just a degree and Vietnam is a communist country.

We will focus on these countries- the four highest earning places for EFL teachers in the world. We will also take a less in depth look at Thailand. Thailand has been added because although you cannot expect to save money working in Thailand it is a very cheap place to live and very popular for it's superior relaxed quality of life. Many people may wish to work for a year in one of the big 4 and then go to Thailand for a year or two with the savings, although being able to get a job there means living even better or for longer.

Japan

Finding Employment

The large chain schools Nova, Geos, ECC, Berlitz and Aeon each hire teachers by the thousands every year. They generally will not hire you if you are already in Japan and do not require you to have TEFL certification.

The Jet program is a very attractive proposition if you can get accepted onto it. It requires you to have a degree (recent graduates are more likely to be accepted), pays 300,000 yen a month, provides free airfare and you can be 110% sure you have a valid work visa as your sponsor is the Japanese government. It is a very popular and competitive program but there are downsides. You do not get to choose where you want to work, so you could find yourself being placed in the middle of nowhere, you are compelled to pay 40,000 yen a month for medical insurance and while your accommodation is provided, you will have to pay the key money.

Apart from through the chains and the Jet program it is easier to find jobs when you are already in Japan, but the high cost of living, especially for accommodation means that it is much wiser to find employment in advance. If however you decide to go and search for jobs on the ground you will be at an advantage over those still overseas and will have no trouble finding employment. If you take this option then I would recommend that you have at least $3000-4000 dollars set aside to fund yourself through until you start getting paid.

The demand for teachers is highest in March and April but teachers are needed in quite high quantities all year round with the possible exception of December and January when things slow down a little. There are however literally hundreds of jobs available every month.

Once you have established yourself in Japan you can earn fairly high wages but it is easier to look for the better paid jobs once you are already in employment in Japan. That means that the internet is a major resource in finding an initial job in Japan. Some of the best job sites for finding employment in Japan are listed below:

http://www.gaijinpot.com/
http://www.jobsinjapan.com/
http://www.ohayosensei.com/

http://www.jalt.org/
http://www.eslcafe.com/
http://www.eltnews.com/home.shtml
http://www.hotjobsjapan.net/

Jobs can also be found in the English language newspapers in Japan: Japan Times *http://www.japantimes.co.jp/*, Kansai Time Out magazine *http://www.kto.co.jp/* and Metropolis *http://www.metropolis.co.jp/*.

The paper edition of The Japan Times has different job adverts. They appear mostly on a Monday but some places (e.g. Hokkaido) have their jobs appear in the Tuesday edition. You can get a subscription for just Mondays sent to you overseas and it will arrive on the Tuesday or Wednesday.

It is easiest to find jobs in the big cities of Tokyo, Osaka and Nagoya or through the large chain schools who have schools throughout the country, but you will find that schools in more out of the way areas advertise in the papers and on the internet.

In my opinion Kumamoto City is worth considering as an alternative to the bigger cities. Its population is just under a million, has an integrated ex-pat/local scene and Mount Aso is less than an hour drive away.

Pay Rates

The minimum you should be getting paid is 250,000 yen a month, slightly more in the bigger cities. Most teachers are easily able to save 75,000-100,000 yen a month on this salary. Tax runs at between 6-9%.

Many schools will offer you a bonus if you complete your one year contract. It is usually between 50,000-100,000 yen. Make sure that this is written into your contract or you may find that the school is able to avoid paying it to you. In addition most employers will either provide health insurance for free or at least heavily subsidize it.

3000-4000 yen is the average price for private lessons an order to legally teach private students you must report all earnings to the tax authorities. Most teachers don't and never get caught.

When teaching private students it is a good idea to give them a "gessha" envelope. These are available in department stores and bookstores and are envelopes with 12 boxes on them. You use them to collect your fees for the whole month in advance, ticking off the boxes when the payment has been made. The Japanese are quite used to using them to pay for services and will know exactly what to do when you give them one. When they agree to take a lesson, give them the envelope which they will bring back when they come to the first lesson. Give back the envelope a week before the next month's fee is due. This gives them a gentle reminder that the next payment is due.

Work Visa

To get a work visa you need to hold a full degree or be able to show that you have substantial (3+ years) experience in a field related to your job offer. If you go for the latter route you need to apply for a Humanities visa. You don't need TEFL certification to obtain a work visa.

You can also enter the country on a working holiday visa (WHV) if you are from the UK, Australia, New Zealand, Canada, France, South Korea or Germany. The visa is valid for 6 months and can be extended one time for another six months, unless you are Australian and then the visa can be extended for an additional 6 months after that. The age limits on the WHV are between your 18th and 31st birthday.

Another option is to enroll on a language or martial arts course and get a student or cultural visa respectively. This will allow you to work legally for 20 hours a week.

If you want to arrive in Japan prior to getting a job offer then you will need to enter on the 3 month tourist visa. Once you have found a job then the employer will begin the visa process which takes around six weeks. In the meantime you are not supposed to work but nearly all schools will start you off straight away. After the visa has been approved you need to get your visa changed at a Japanese embassy outside the country which will mean a visa run to Seoul in South Korea which wont take longer than 2 days.

Accommodation

The chain schools will all arrange accommodation for you. Living rooms and bedrooms in Japan are very small; a typical room will only be 110 square feet. Don't expect to find regular beds in Japan. All apartments will instead have futons. Many teachers are unused to sleeping on the floor and find that they need extra foam padding which is available from most department stores.

Many non-chain school employers will provide you with housing or subsidize your rent. Your school should be the one to pay the landlord their "key money" and all the other customary "gifts". Key money is basically your deposit.

If your accommodation is not provided then your will almost certainly have to stay in a "gaijin house" which is a fairly cheap long-stay hostel for foreigners for several months. Expect to pay 50,000-80,000 Yen a month, plus a refundable 25,000 Yen deposit. You can find a list of the ones in Tokyo in the Tokyo Journal or search for the term on a search engine for the location you are intending to move to.

83

When you are ready to rent an apartment be prepared for a lot of haste. If your school is well established and doesn't provide accommodation then they may already have a good relationship with real estate agents which can make the process a lot smoother… it will still be a pain though!

You can't deal with landlords directly; you have to go through real estate agents. The first problem is that many landlords issue a "no foreigners" request to their agents. The likelihood is that you will get turned down many, many times before you find an apartment that you, as a foreigner, can rent.

Next you need a guarantor. This has to be a Japanese national with a good credit history. Your school should be willing to act as your guarantor. Not all agents will require that you have a guarantor so it is worth checking with them, but most do, those that don't will often require you to pay for your entire stay upfront!

Finally you need money… a lot of money! You need to pay the equivalent of one month's rent as a holding fee which will be refunded when you sign contracts. The real estate agent will charge you one month's rent as their fee. The Key money is usually 2-3 months rent, is often 4 in Tokyo but can be as high as 6! Technically you are meant to get this back when you leave but in practice this money is earmarked for maintenance and upkeep, repainting and the like of this and other properties and even if you leave the apartment looking brand new you will be very lucky to see any of your deposit back. If this wasn't bad enough you also have to give the landlord a compulsory "gift" which is usually 2 months rent.

Apartments in Tokyo and other large cities can be had at 40,000-60,000 Yen a month at the low end of the scale.

House and apartment sizes are not measured in feet or meters but by "tatami" mat size. A single tatami is 1.8 meters by 90 cm. Most apartments aren't actually covered in tatami mats but if yours is then make sure you point out any damage before you sign the contract. If you don't then you will be charged for them and they are expensive.

South Korea

The Best and the Worst

Korea is the best place for new English teachers to start out. All you need is a full degree and to be born in an English speaking country. It also provides some of the best pay when you consider that accommodation is paid for- accommodation and education being the two biggest expenses for Koreans- flights are paid for, cost of living is low, tax is low and wages are reasonable (approximately US$2,000 a month).

Korea is also the worst place to be a teacher if you get a job at a bad school. So bad that the US foreign office issued a warning to their nationals to robustly research who they took a job with as they would be unable to help them in any dispute.

Korea does have a bad reputation and there are bad schools out there. Don't be frightened off though.

Many, many more people have good experiences teaching English in Korea than those who have bad experiences. The following section especially might put you off South Korea- don't let it! These are worst case scenario coping tactics and don't reflect the majority of schools or bosses.

Avoiding corruption

Firstly, research the school you have been offered a job by (or the school the recruiter wants to place you in). If it is a brand new school I would avoid it as it is an unproven commodity and the owner could go bust. Type the schools name in quotation brackets into a search engine "like this" and see what comes up, maybe add words like "Korea", "teach", "blacklist". Ask to speak and have the email addresses of both current and past teachers who can give you an honest assessment of the school and the boss.

Never, ever give your passport to the school. If they need to take it to immigration then go with them and take it yourself- you will need to be there anyway to sign forms etc.

Don't ever lose your temper or argue with your boss. There is no point, they will see it as disrespect and be more likely to treat you badly, and it won't get you anywhere as the boss is always in a stronger position than you. If there is evidence then your case will be upheld but if it is your word vs. that of a Korean then the Koreans word wins.

By law if the schools don't have money they don't have

to pay you until they are able! If this happens then again, the most important thing to remember is not to blow up or get angry. Just keep nagging them in a very respectful but persistent way, explaining you need the money, have student loans to pay off or are supporting a non-existent grandmother who has medical bills.

If you haven't been paid for a significant amount of time then without warning them beforehand simply stop teaching! Never, ever threaten or blackmail your boss, but when you are confronted tell them (calmly) that you will start teaching again when you are paid what you are owed- money will magically appear in your account!

Your boss may come to you with unreasonable demands- overtime that you don't want to do or is unpaid, criticism of your teaching style or generally nagging you. Again, never get cross. You can just say "no", they will probably look at you funnily and ask again, the key is to neither get worn into submission, nor loose your temper- a quick grin and "I said no, why are you asking again? Maybe I should work for someone who understands English" if said in the right way will often get the desired response. If not, and it's something like overtime, just keep reminding the boss what it says in your contract. They will hate it but there's not a lot they can do about it. If it's something like teaching style or something that you can't change just agree with them and do it your own way anyway- this usually works wonders!

89

Job Before vs. Job on the Ground

Having your airfare paid for is one of the huge perks of working in South Korea and is usually only available if you have applied outside the country. If you are incredibly smooth you may be able to negotiate the price of an air ticket into your contract if you are already in Korea but most are not able to.

The paid airfare is one reason why many people choose South Korea in the first place. Obviously it is a huge advantage, and coupled with accommodation being available for you from the first day can be good reasons to arrange employment outside of the country (not to mention that you won't have to complete the visa run).

Many longer time teachers in Korea recommend that if you are able to you should look for jobs within the country, especially if you already have some experience. The reasons for this is that you are able to check out your employer more thoroughly, see the accommodation for yourself and talk to current foreign teachers at the school often outside settings where you can be overheard and they will give you an honest assessment. You will have to pay your own airfare, find accommodation until you find employment and do the visa run though.

The easiest and by far the most common way to find jobs in Korea is on the internet. Use the general internet job board resources given earlier on although you only really need to use Dave's Café to find more than enough jobs in Korea. Do make sure you ask them all the right questions before flying out though!

Pay Scale

The average minimum wage you should be looking for even without any experience is around 1.7 million Won as long as accommodation is provided. At the upper levels 2.3 million Won would be an exceptionally good wage if you've never taught before. In the big cities like Seoul you should really look for a starting salary of at least 2 million Won. Many schools will also pay for your airfare. Some of them will buy the airfare for you, most will require you to pay for the airfare and then reimburse you on arrival. Don't assume that "on arrival" actually means on arrival!

Most schools require you to work for a month first and reimburse your fare with your first pay-packet. The reason they do this is that otherwise savvy travelers would apply for jobs just to get the airfare to Asia and then skip town. Some schools may want to wait until the end of your contact before reimbursing you the cost of your airplane ticket. I would strongly suggest that you do not allow this to happen, and maybe even have when you will be repaid the cost of the ticket written into your contract; a month is a fair compromise.

In addition you have an end of contract bonus written into your contact as part of Korean law. This could vary but will usually be one month's wages. Some disreputable schools may try to dismiss you before you reach the end of your contract to avoid paying especially if they still owe you airfare. It is always wise never to start slacking off because you are nearing the end of your contract and give them opportunity to do so.

Once accommodation is dealt with then that is the largest expensive out of the way. Most people manage to live off of 700,000 Won without being frugal at all but living very well meaning that you can save 1,000,000+ won a month fairly easily.

Payment will happen in one of two ways, either directly into your Korean bank account or more commonly in cash. If at all possible I would recommend trying to get the school to deposit the money in your bank account as then there can be no possibility of the wages being short-changed!

Teaching private students is illegal in South Korea however so long as you are careful and sensible there is realistically very little chance of getting caught.

You can generally earn 30,000-60,000 won an hour and many teachers earn up to $500 a month. Teachers who leave your school may have groups of private students who will need a new teacher, otherwise you can get started when you are approached- and you will be, everywhere- by people asking if you will teach them or their kids.

Contracts

The "bonus" of an extra months wage if you complete your contract is not a bonus at all but a recruitment of the Korean government which you are legally entitled to.

If you decide not to stay with the school and fail to get a release form then you are not allowed to teach in Korea until the contract you signed expires, on top of this the school owner may try to get you blacklisted from being allowed to work in Korea again if you just storm out. Consider that whenever a teacher breaks their contract it costs the school up to $5,000 to replace them, not to mention the disruption it causes the students.

If you do want to get released from your contract then you need to do one of two things- either tell your boss that you want to be released but you will wait until a replacement is found (the problem is they may say no), or you may have to lie.

Korea has a strong family values system and telling them that a close relative has died and you need to console your family will usually get them to agree that you can leave. You can then try and get a letter of release. If your boss then tells you that you don't need one as your not coming back to Korea you will need to try and tell them that Korean immigration won't allow you to leave the country without one.

Other Money Issues

All you need to open a local bank account is a passport.
It would be a good idea to bank with the same bank as
the other foreign teachers at your school as they will be
able to help you and the bank will hopefully be used to
dealing with English speaking clients. If not then one of
the Korean teachers should be able to help you find a
bank that has people used to dealing with foreigners.
They are all pretty much the same anyway.

You can transfer money overseas from your bank
however you are technically limited to sending 60% of
your salary overseas. Many banks ignore this and do
not mark your passport when you transfer money; some
allow you to send 80% etc.

An alternative option is to take a trip across to Thailand
having converted your money to dollars and to send
from a western union branch there as they will not limit
the amount you can send home.

Most ATM's are not 24 hour but close around 11pm,
and lots of places only accept cash only and not debit or
credit cards. The Won's exchange rate fluctuates (you
can check its current status here) but a good rule of

thumb is 1,000 Won = US$1.

Income tax is about 4% of your salary. Some employers also take out the national pension plan contribution (4.5%) and national heath insurance premium (2%), but most exclude the pension plan if not both.

Accommodation

Accommodation in South Korea can be fairly expensive, especially in Seoul but most positions will offer you free accommodation as part of your package. Sometimes it will be close to the school and other times might require a commute.

Traveling will be especially likely if you work in Seoul or another big city. Accommodation offered is usually either in a shared apartment or a single apartment and should be specified before the contract is signed.

What your apartment is like depends a lot on the luck of the draw; if you are already in Korea then you should see where you will be living before agreeing to teach for the school. If not you may be able to get the school to send you photographs of it beforehand.

Visa Requirements

In order to teach in South Korea you must be in position of a valid visa. There are two things that are needed in order to get a visa; a college degree and an offer of employment. It is possible to enter on a tourist visa and secure potential employment. If this route is taken then after the offer of employment you must leave South Korea and re-enter on your work visa, this almost certainly means flying to Japan on the infamous "visa run". If you decide to stay in South Korea, even if you stay with the same school, then you must complete this run every time your contract is renewed or you take up a new contract. Almost universally the length of employment will be one year due to visa regulations.

There is no limitation to the amount of times you can apply for a work visa and they are almost always granted if a school is willing to employ you and they verify you have a degree. It is worth noting that it is NOT the South Korean government who verify your degree credentials. It is the employer's job to verify that you do indeed hold a degree and inform the government that they have seen them. Many employers are very lax in this area if you are already in South Korea and they like the look of you, especially if they are told that the certification is overseas. If they know that you don't have a degree they may use that to terminate your contract early to avoid paying you bonuses and airfare re-imbursement secure in the knowledge that you won't make a fuss and risk deportation.

If applying from overseas many schools or recruiters acting on behalf of schools will ask you to send your original degree certificate and sometimes the transcripts to them for verification. This should always be sent by recordable delivery like Fed-Ex. This in particular is where "life experience" degrees come in very handy-lots of schools and recruiters will only check that the certificates look acceptable and maybe check with the institution that you are a graduate there. A few especially hard cases (usually western with advanced degrees) may dig a little further and might reject your application on this basis. This only means that you cannot use that school or recruiter; there are thousands of English Language schools in South Korea. They will send back the accreditation and put in a visa application request for you with the government confirming their interest in employing you and confirming that they have seen your degree proof.

As of March 2008 all teachers will also have to jump through several more hoops in order to get a visa. This is due mainly to a highly publicized case of a teacher being exposed as a convicted western pedophile. The major changes are that in order to get a visa you will need to have a medical check (those infected with the HIV virus will not be granted a visa) and also provide a recent criminal record check from your home country. In addition to this there will also be an interview at your nearest Korean consulate and a further interview once you land in Korea at which, technically, they could revoke your visa. It is very unlikely in practice that this would happen and there is already talk of replacing the interview in Korea with e-interviews over the internet.

Be Aware

South Koreans tend to be very proud of Korea. They will be quite happy to argue that South Korea is the only country in the world that has four seasons, that Korea invented the printing press (and anything else you can imagine), that the Korean language is superior to any other and that anything Korean is better than anything foreign. Any potential reasoning against this e.g. that Brazil are better at soccer than them is met either with blank denial of the obvious or with a victim mentality that requires you to agree that if there were a level playing field Korea is superior.

The Asian "face saving" mentality is in full play and it is considered rude to show up others especially your elders by showing them to be wrong, even if they are lying or being blatantly dishonest. This respect extends to doing whatever the boss says and can cause problems between western English language teachers and the schools if they are not aware of it. Compared to the Korean teachers, English teachers get treated very well and this should be remembered and cause you not to go into melt down mode when faced with unreasonable demands but instead deal with it in a measured response. It is not unusual for head teachers to scream at Korean teachers and for them to accept it, but this behavior is not seen as acceptable to English language teachers. They may however make unreasonable demands or deny something had been agreed. This can usually be overcome if the teacher keeps a cool head and is firm in stating holding their position without being rude. This doesn't happen everywhere but it is more blatant in Korea than the West even though many bosses still "ask" workers to stay late or work weekends with no intention that they would get told no.

South Korea is a mix of Confucianism and Christianity. 25% of Koreans are Christian and the country even boasts the world's largest congregation (the 800,000 member full gospel church of the Rev Yoggi Cho). Even so there is a huge drinking culture. Often Koreans are not only pressed to go to after work drinks but also forced to drink huge amounts where "no" is not an acceptable answer. Foreign teachers are expected to come at least occasionally but unlike their Korean counterparts can decline drinks without too much trouble by falling back on medical conditions or Christianity as to why they're not getting drunk. This does mean that it is not outside the realms of probability that you may see men in suits at 6 or 7am sleeping on park benches suddenly waking up, wiping the vomit from themselves and going to work!

Eating is a habit that many foreigners find annoying. It is fairly common to find that Koreans do not eat with their mouths closed and will often snort like pigs (literally) while eating. They are often aware that Westerners find this disgusting, but as they may be willing to point out- you're in Korea now. If you do any of these things though they may well tell you to stop being rude and that you should eat like a Korean! Sometimes this is said tongue in cheek but sometimes they really do have blinkers on.

Among other things that may offend you is the constant spiting on the side walk and the way that strangers will bump you, push you out of their way and cut in line before you. These instances often infuriate recently graduated liberal arts majors who have come out of a fluffy politically correct environment to the point that they are ready to leave forever. I suggest when you are cut in a line that you cut in front of them, preferably pushing them out of the way and spitting at their feet while you do so… when in Rome!

Taiwan

Where to Teach

You will most likely arrive in Taiwan by flying into Taipei. There are a lot of schools in Taipei but they actually tend to pay less than schools elsewhere. As a rule of thumb, northern Taiwan is more crowded and expensive. Taipei's cost of living has been estimated as being as much as 50-100% greater than on the rest of the Island and it can also rain for weeks on end and be very cold in winter.

If you are willing to go to the smaller towns, especially in the south, then the schools will often bend over backwards to help you as most of the English teachers never leave Taipei. The advantages include that while a two bedroom apartment in Taipei costs NT$10,000 a month you can get a five bedroom house with a garden in Kaohsiung for that price. Prices vary enormously all over the island and you can usually find something within your price range.

Taipei is the cleanest, safest and most convenient city in Taiwan to live in though. If you do decide on Taipei then you should avoid living in the city centre or the south-western suburbs.

Tienmu is where most foreigners live and although everyone there speaks English, it is expensive and can be a congested journey to downtown. Instead you should look to the northern or south-western suburbs. Consider Mucha, Yung Ho or Neihu. Possibly the best place to live here is in nearby Tamshui which is only a quarter of an hour metro ride to Taipei. It has a more relaxed atmosphere, is on the Ocean and yet is near enough to the city to commute into work.

Finding Employment

It is easy to find work over the net. One big advantage of finding a job before you get here is that if it is a salaried position then you sometimes get a refund for a one-way air ticket. It is usually impossible to negotiate that once you are here on the ground.

Salaried jobs will guarantee you an income but will often have a 30 hour week, while hourly contracts are required to be for at least 14 hours to be legal.

You need to make sure that when a school offers you 20 hours or 25 hours a week on an hourly contract that they will actually follow through. The only way to do this is to have a minimum paid hours a week put in your contract. This is because schools in Taiwan are notorious for not always being able to deliver the hours they promised.

Conversely you need to also have a maximum hours clause put in your contract. This is because in the busy periods schools in Taiwan that have offered 25 hour weeks have forced teachers to work 50 hour weeks and then cut the hours to 10 hours a week in the downtimes! This is far too long (and not long enough in the down time).

Always ask how much preparation and traveling time (if applicable) you are expected to do. It is not unheard of for Taiwanese school owners to try and get naïve new teachers to do up to 10 hours of unpaid work a week because they don't know any better.

Other Taiwan specific questions to ask the school are: Do they withhold any part of the first months pay? This is illegal but many schools do so. Likewise check that they won't be giving you a lower than expected "training wage" for the first three months. If the school is outside of Taipei then the school should be willing to help you get a scooter, many schools will provide one as part of the employment package if you ask for it. Also raise the issue of air fare if you are applying from overseas. Many schools in Taiwan now offer re-imbursement of a one way ticket or a free plane ticket when recruiting from overseas. This needs to be negotiated if not offered and you need to make sure that the "free" airline ticket isn't going to be deducted from your pay.

As you can now legally work at two different schools I would recommend you do so as this gives you more leverage, and protects you against a school folding, becoming over demanding etc. Make the days you are available for work clear and in your contract. This will make it easier to get a second job and then first school can't accuse you of breaking your contract, which would result in your work visa getting revoked as they are the sponsoring employer. However don't tell your potential employer about your intention to work elsewhere as they may be reluctant to hire you. If you're stuck for an excuse to why you need certain days or times off then the best one is that you are studying Chinese.

While the recruiters who work for specific school advertising online are usually ok to use I would avoid the Taiwanese based recruiters who charge you a fee for their services. They have a very bad reputation and are not above tricking you into working illegally. Besides if you are already in Taiwan then there is no need to use them.

Stepping of the plane and into a job in Taiwan is very easy. Jobs are advertised in all three of the major daily English language newspapers (The China Post, Taipei Times and Taiwan News). Rent a scooter when looking for jobs as it will make things a lot easier. The hostel managers are often a good source of information about which schools are looking to employ teachers, and notice boards in ex-pat hangouts will always have lots of job adverts on them. Especially good in Taiwan are in ex-pat grocery stores. Also check out the notice boards at the Mandarin Hostel, Mandarin Training Centre, and the Taipei Hostel which are a couple of blocks away from the main station in Taipei. Just because you are already in Taiwan doesn't mean that you should forsake the internet; follow up on adverts posted on ***http://www.tealit.com/*** and Dave's Café. Use the fact that you are already in the country to your advantage both with getting the job and the pay/benefits you can negotiate. If the school is legal then it will have a picture of the owner and an official looking document in a prominent place. If you can't see one then don't take the job as it's an illegal and probably short lived, school.

You can't buy a mobile phone without an ARC which is a recent development. Obviously this makes it more difficult if you've given your CV to a school and they want to contact you. I would consider using the Taiwanese eBay site, which is an official eBay site, to buy a mobile phone and sim card before going.

The best time to come to Taiwan is August to early September as this is when the new school year starts and many teachers return to the USA and UK to grad school. The next best time to arrive is January. The reality is though that few teachers with a Celta type qualification will experience problems finding work on the ground whenever they arrive. As far as tax is concerned though, it is best to arrive before the 30th June. If you are in Taiwan for 183 days in the tax year then the following December you receive a refund meaning that you effectively pay 13% tax.

Pay Rates

Most first year teachers can expect to earn NT$55-60,000 a month. NT$400-600 an hour is the usual pay scale for hourly contracts. You can negotiate private lessons from NT$600-1000 an hour. Technically they are illegal but as long as your employer either doesn't mind or doesn't find out then you should be fine.

A maximum of 6% of your wage is taken in National Health Insurance premiums. These are compulsory and while you do not receive free healthcare it is nonetheless very cheap and usually administrated by American trained healthcare professionals.

The tax year in Taiwan runs from Jan 1st to Dec 31st. For the first 183 days of the first tax year you are in Taiwan you will be taxed at 20%. After you have been in Taiwan for a total of 183 days- as long as it is the same tax year- your tax goes down, typically to 13%. You can claim back the amount you overpaid during the initial 183 days the following May and can expect to receive it around November time. If you have been in Taiwan for a total of 183 days or more the previous year then the tax rate will not go back up to 20%.

Work Visa

If you haven't already got a job arranged before coming over then you will need to arrive on a visitor's visa, find work and get the school to sponsor their work visa. Most teachers who arrived first and then looked for a job work for the schools that are sponsoring them while they wait for their visa to be processed; this is technically illegal, although it is very rare for anyone to get into trouble by doing so.

Apply for visitor visa even if your country allows you to arrive on the visa wavier program because the visa will allow you to stay in the country long enough to find a job and apply for an ARC without having to do a visa run.

The school will apply for your work visa. Most schools don't realize this but a degree is not needed for a work visa. However, if you don't have a degree then you need a two year college diploma and a tesol certificate that is of Celta standard.

For the work visa you need copies of your degree and transcripts provided by your college and they need to be stamped by your local Taiwanese representative office. It is best to get this done before you go.

When you have your work visa you need to apply for your ARC (Alien Residents Certificate). The school should help you with this. You will need the card as a form of ID.

The work permit lets you legally work at two jobs; the school that sponsored you and one (and only one) other. Some schools don't care if you work elsewhere or teach privately and some do. The second school needs to apply to be put on your ARC.

If you decide to leave your school and they are happy to let you go then technically you can transfer your ARC to another school. In reality though this is a very rare occurrence even if you have left on good terms. If you want to continue teaching in Taiwan it is imperative that you obtain a release letter from your old school. You will still have to leave Taiwan and re-enter on a new visitor visa for your new school to apply for a new ARC and work visa but they will need the letter of release or you will not be granted a work visa. If they let the CLA know that you left without giving notice then you may find yourself blacklisted and unable to get a new work visa when your new school applies for one on your behalf.

If and when you have been in Taiwan for several years then you can apply for the "open visa" which allows you to work in an unlimited number of jobs, which obviously makes life a lot easier.

If you really can't get a work visa, perhaps because you have no degree, then the best bet to work illegally is to apply for a five year multi-entry visa and when asked why you need one to claim it is for business purposes. You need to create an impressive looking business card with an important sounding title for yourself. Next you should get a letter from a Taiwanese business inviting you to go and see their products.

These are easy to obtain, and most companies will send you one without any bother. Look up potential companies on a search engine, but some of the best to approach are Acer and Evergreen. If you want to go all out then buy tickets to an international trade show and time your arrival to just before it starts. It is technically a tourist visa but you must specifically say it is for business purposes. That way you can extend it at a travel agent's in Taiwan for up to six months before you need to do a visa run.

Accommodation

When arriving in Taiwan without a job and accommodation already arranged it is best to check into a hostel for a month or so and then rent an apartment. It is worth considering renting a Tao Fang in the short term. They are one bedroom apartments that usually come fully furnished and not require a huge deposit. Hostels are cheaper than hotels, but they can be cramped and dirty. They are also technically illegal so they don't advertise themselves; you need to ask around to find out where they are.

Apart from getting your school to help you look for housing- some schools will even offer you housing as part of the deal, especially if they recruited you from overseas- the best places to look are where foreigners get together, American international schools and missionary schools.

For cheap housing you could try the Tsui Mama service that usually caters to students. Other agents advertise in the local English language newspapers.

Alternatively, if you have someone with you who speaks Chinese then go round the area you would like to move to and look out for red and yellow signs on notice boards and telegraph poles. These advertise property available to rent and also for sale, but it never hurts to ask if property advertised for sale is available to rent.

Also keep a look out for empty houses and ask the neighbors how to contact the owners and if it's available to rent. This is probably the best method as many people have given up trying to find people to rent their houses and a good price can be negotiated. For instance it's estimated that up to half of all houses in Taichung are empty! A standard deposit is two months rent along with a months rent in advance.

If you rent an apartment then it is worthwhile going for one in a block that has at least 13 floors. All 13 floor plus apartment blocks are built in compliance with strict earthquake prevention regulations but 12 floor and under blocks have much more lax building regulations.

Also don't rent a place near a military base or a temple. Areas around military bases suffer high crime and temples let off fireworks until 3am on a semi-regular bases. Check that all the windows, doors and balconies on the house you rent have bars on and that the bars have an exit hatch in case of a fire.

116

Taiwan Specifics

Illegal is a relative term in Taiwan. There is illegal, as
in murder, that really is illegal and then there is
technically illegal. I can guarantee that if you stay in
Taiwan for more than three months you will have
technically broken the law multiple times. Way back in
2004 the Taiwanese government banned foreign
teachers from working in kindergartens. Everyone
ignored the new law even though occasionally they did
try to enforce it in Taipei. Another example of
Taiwanese nonsense laws is regarding public high
schools. They are allowed, encouraged by the
government even, to employ foreign teachers but they
are not allowed to apply for work visas for them! They
get round this by paying a private language centre to
get their teachers work visa (so the teacher legally isn't
employed by them). This of course is technically illegal
even though the government publicly says it wants
more foreign teachers in its high schools!

Taiwanese tend to be reluctant to show anger or
frustration. It is important for you to realize that what
you would think of as an acceptable show of mild
impatience can be significantly overestimated by
Taiwanese and they will often think that it's intended

toward them personally.

This means that when dealing with problems with your school or boss remember to be calm. Don't do anything that causes them to think you have "lost face" or you will find it harder to rectify the problem. In turn, don't make your employer loose face. While being firm and clear what you will and won't accept, try to word things in a way that will let them suggest the outcome you want and show how gracious they are. If this doesn't work then start getting blunter, but always give them the option of saving face wherever possible no matter how farcical it seems as you're not really giving them any choice!

Taiwanese often regard everything on the grade-curve mentality. If someone is successful that means someone else is a failure. This means that if you get a rise, bonus or get praised by your students then your Taiwanese co-workers may well see this as you gaining at their expense and start to try to go after you. The Taiwanese sometimes seem to live to engage in office politics but it is better to just try and ignore it. It won't go away but after a while it won't affect you much anymore.

Vietnam

Where to Teach?

The two main cities that most of the work in Vietnam is available are Ho Chi Minh City (also known as HCMC or Saigon) and Hanoi. It is sometimes possible to find work in the language schools in some of the smaller cities like Hai Phong, Can Tho, Nha Trang, Vung Tau and Da Nang, but both the hours available and the pay will be much less.

If you do want to try somewhere smaller then I would recommend that you initially find work in HCMC or Hanoi and get leads from teachers and language schools in the city, visiting prospective cities when you have time off to get a better idea of teaching options there.

It is unlikely that you will find a language school in Vietnam that will give you enough hours to work exclusively for them, although a willingness to work

Saturdays and Sundays will increase your chances.

Most teachers opt to work for two or more schools and this is one country in which the schools won't mind you doing this. It is quite easy to work full time (25 hours per week) year round with the exception of during Tet.

Teachers normally work close to where they live, so it makes sense to work for several schools close together and not spread throughout the city.

Finding Employment

Very, very few language schools in Vietnam advertise on the internet and the ones that do will usually will only talk with people who have extensive qualifications and experience. Not to mention that if they don't need teachers or are not 100% convinced about you by your CV then they will ignore your emails to them. This means that to find a job you realistically need to travel to Vietnam and look for work there.

I would advise that you take the first job that is offered you. The big chains, Language Link and The British Council should be the first attempts. Early afternoon is the best time to visit schools.

It is best to look and act professionally in Vietnam. It's too hot to wear a suit but business shirts and tie for males and smart casual for females is required. You may find work if you have long hair, earrings (male) and visible tattoos but these things aren't really approved of. The look to avoid is that of a backpacker as the students will give you less respect and the pay you will be offered will be a lot lower. In fact not having a degree sometimes won't matter if you look the part and are willing to work with small kids.

There may be some initial reluctance to hire Asian looking teachers at anything more than the rates they pay local teachers, especially if you or your family originally came from Vietnam. Despite this there are many Asian looking teachers on the same pay as the school's Caucasian teachers so it is worth persevering. One piece of advice to Viet Kieu is never to use Vietnamese in the classroom or to admit knowing it to the school administrators or you risk being seen as not a real native English speaker.

While the need for teachers in Vietnam means that anyone can get a job there is very little ageism regarding teachers in Vietnam. If anything older teachers are more sought after than young (35 and under) teachers and shown more respect in the classroom by the students.

When you have a job be professional, work hard and care about teaching as the Vietnamese have a lot of respect for committed teachers. If you do a good job then you will get approached outside the school about teaching private lessons. I would get some business cards and hand them out to everyone as it is culturally acceptable, even normal here. Let some of these people know that you are looking for a better job, keep networking and you will start to be offered positions that are not advertised anywhere, as the better paying schools can choose to approach teachers rather than the other way round.

Also hand out the business cards while handing out your CV to schools as these tend to get stapled together and also sometimes kept if there are no teacher vacancies whereas CV's often aren't kept. If you put the mobile phone number in a bold font then this also increases the response.

Making contacts is an important aspect to improve your life and job in Vietnam. This may be true to a certain extent in other countries but it really is the single biggest way here. As has been said already; the best jobs are never advertised or offered to people looking for work, it happens the other way round here!

If you get to know Vietnamese people then they will introduce you to people and want to show you different places. Everything comes down to knowing something here; better paying/lower hour jobs, cheaper but better accommodation etc. It tends to be when the locals realize that you are not here as a tourist for a couple of months that doors start opening, they often don't want to invest in or recommend people that will be critical of their culture and country and are looking to leave fairly soon. Strange huh?

Pay Rates

The VND is pegged to the US Dollar and so will fluctuate with currencies like the Euro or Pound Sterling but not the US Dollar.

Pay rates depend on the type of school you work for. At the lower end (US$10 an hour) the schools will generally hire anyone who speaks English, will have photocopies of textbooks, no air conditioning, poor facilities but will normally treat you very well as they are happy to have native speakers working for them. These will almost always be run by Vietnamese natives.

The top end employers pay between US$15-20 an hour and generally require a degree, Celta or equivalent and 3 years teaching experience. Employers like this are The British Council, RMIT Vietnam and ACET. These jobs are obviously more difficult to come by and the facilities and standards are both very high.

Most teachers in Vietnam are paid US$10-15 and employed by a mid tier language school. The schools prefer experienced teachers if possible but they are usually willing to give newcomers a go if they hold TEFL qualifications and look professional, especially if they need staff.

US$12 is the least you should accept if you have experience or a TEFL qualification (US$14 for night hours). It is easier to find work for weekend and night hours, so if a school is unable to also offer daytime teaching hours in return then you should negotiate your wage up. Negotiation is important in Vietnam regarding hours and pay because many of the schools will often offer you little in the expectation that you will negotiate up or accept the first offer as you don't know better!

Backpackers (who look and act like backpackers rather than professionals) can and do get employment but they are usually stuck at the US$6-10 mark. After a month or two and having let the school see that you are a decent teacher and reliable, if you are earning US$12 an hour it is more than possible to negotiate up to US$14 an hour.

A good benchmark for private lesson rates is between US$20-25 an hour.

You can live off US$500-700 a month as long as you aren't a heavy drinker and this means that you can save US$500-$1000 a month quite easily.

Not all schools tax correctly! In general you should expect to get taxed at a whopping 25% for your first 6 months! Vietnamese law requires this to be refunded after 6 months. If you have a contract then you can expect to pay the following per school, per month: Up to 8 Million VND (aprox US$550) isn't taxable; from 8 million VND to 20 million VND (approx US$1300) is taxed at 10%; from 20 million to 40 million VND (aprox US$2600) is taxed at 20%.

Non-contracted teachers are usually assessed at 10% of anything over 500,000 VND (aprox US$325) but if the school pays the teachers tax liability then the tax rate is negotiable!

Bank Accounts

When opening a bank account you will need to prove where the initial money deposited came from. If it is your salary then you will need a letter from the school stating how much money you've earned before you can deposit it. Lots of schools don't pay you straight into you're bank account but this may be able to be negotiated.

Most employers are not legally allowed to pay you in foreign currency. If however your employer is allowed to do so then taking a copy of the contract to the Vietcombank should allow you to get a dollar account. The Vietcombank allows you to transfer that money back home. Even if you get paid by VND then the banks are legally allowed to change it into foreign currency and transfer it out, but many choose not to do so.

You are legally only allowed to take US$7,000 out of the country per year via customs. If you have more than this on you when you at a border then they will confiscate the excess, in practice they often don't check but there is that risk.

If you ask the banks to transfer money out of the country you will most likely be told that you can't transfer money to another country anywhere in Vietnam. As previously stated this is actually false it's just that most banks won't do it for you. Those that do will require proof that you earned the money legally. This needs to be your teaching contract and wage slips so if you are teaching privately then this won't count. Then they will mark off the amount on the yellow slip in your passport off of the US$7,000 amount. One way round this is to "loose" the yellow slip as often happens anyway. It is a pain to get it replaced but it can be done because so many people legitimately loose it every year.

Shinhan Vina (a Korean Bank) will transfer money you can show you have paid tax on if you also have a contract and payslips and will do so without writing any amount on the yellow slip.

Work Visa

To get a work permit you need a CV, Degree and/or Tefl Certificate (Celta level), Police check (Vietnam and your home country), 3 passport sized photos and a medical report from the hospital. All schools are required by HCMC law to pay all expenses due to obtaining and registering the work permit. You do need the paperwork listed and if the school fills out the paperwork correctly then the work visa lasts for three years and allows you to work for any school.

Don't get stuck with a one-school work visa, negotiate heavily on this aspect as some schools will try and put in your contract that you can only work for them and that they can revoke your visa if you leave the school. Don't sign a contract like this until they take those clauses out.

I'd highly recommend getting the police check from your home country before you leave as it can sometimes be quite difficult obtaining one from Vietnam. Americans need a full national FBI check. It's worthwhile to request some copies of your degree from your university as you may well loose the original copy sometime during the work visa application process (they do usually turn up though).

You can get into the country initially with a one month tourist visa and you don't need an onward ticket if you come on a tourist visa. As long as your contract with the schools are under 3 months then you don't need to get a work permit. You would get a 3 month renewable Business visa. You do not need to leave Vietnam to get your visa renewed. Most travel agents will renew you visa for an extra five and a half months for around US$120. You don't need a tefl certificate to teach in Vietnam if you go the 3 month, non-working visa route, although some school will require one, but it will be a big plus as any certificate is seen as valuable, more valuable than years of experience without a certificate.

If you live in Vietnam for more than two or three years you will eventually meet all sorts of government and police officials that are able to deal with any bureaucratic problems regarding residency permits should you want to go down that route.

Accommodation

When you first arrive in Vietnam your best bet for accommodation is in the tourist/backpacker quarter of Hanoi or HCMC. The Lonely Planet guides will have a list of hotels and it's not hard to find a decent room with air-con and cable TV for less than US$10 a night. Once you are ready to look for longer term accommodation you can rent an apartment for about US$250 a month or a house for between US$250-600 a month.

When you rent an "apartment" be aware that it will usually mean that you are renting one or two rooms (and a bathroom) in a house. Often you will not be given a front door key which means that if you come back late at night you may have to wake people up in order to get in! You will need to pay a bond of around two to six months rent upfront. When you give your notice to the landlord you can stop paying rent and after you've left the landlord will keep the remaining bond to cover any damages or outstanding bills before returning the remainder. Tenants are required to register their accommodation with the local police station.

Most westerners in HCMC live in District 1 in the backpacker quarter (the De Tham/Pham Ngu Lao area) or the "Foreigner Ghetto" (around the corner of Le Thanh Ton and Thai Van Lung). These are the areas you will find most of the Western fast food places, restaurants, bars and ex-pat hangouts. If you move outside District 1 then things get a lot cheaper and quieter. The best places to move into are districts that are close to District 1 as they will be near enough to the schools. These would be Districts 3, 5 and 10, Phu Nhuan District and the Binh Thanh District. The Hanoi suburbs of Ba Dinh/West Lake are fairly reasonable for teachers.

If you are not Vietnamese or have Vietnamese ancestry then you currently can't buy property here. This may change in the future due to Vietnam joining the WTO. There are certain apartment buildings in HCMC and Hanoi that foreigners can rent long term (up to 30 years).

Corruption

The TEFL community in HCMC is relatively small at less than a thousand with fewer still in Hanoi and this helps to regulate the language schools. If a school starts behaving unethically then you will here about it fairly quickly (especially if you tell someone you've just been offered a job there), this has had a knock on effect of causing the TEFL work conditions and attitudes of employers to be very good and you are not nearly as likely to get an employer trying to rip you off as in some other Asian countries (cough*southkorea*cough).

Bribes are a common way of doing things here, red tape and seemingly impossible situations can be solved very quickly indeed. Alternatively if you can't bring yourself to pay the suggested extra "fee", then lots of situations that shouldn't be complicated can suddenly take hours, days or maybe never!

Crime

Violent crime is rare in Vietnam but petty crime can be fairly common. The pickpockets here can be very good and bag snatching isn't unheard but much of it can be minimized by using the same precautions you would use in any large city worldwide.

Motorbike thieves do need to be watched out for though. They will try to snatch something as they ride past. Purses shouldn't be worn on the shoulder but across the body to avoid them getting snatched. Having said that if you are non-Asian then you are much less likely to be the victim of a robbery. Although you will usually have more money than a Vietnamese, the police crack down much more on attacks on foreigners because they don't want Vietnam to be seen as a dangerous place for tourists (and their money) to visit!

That said teachers do find themselves the victims of motorcycle thieves on occasion. If robbed you should go directly to the local police station. You need to tell them that you will be very appreciative if they can get your belongings back. Yes that does mean that they will expect money! They are not always able to get all of your stuff back, but they should be able to recover any documents, passports etc. In order to get other items back you may be required to pay a "gift".

Also in HCMC there are police who wear khaki instead of green uniforms, these are the tourist police who generally patrol where tourists may be. They actually have the authority to beat criminals who prey on tourists with their billy clubs!

Transport

Buses are the cheapest and most inconvenient way of getting round HCMC and Hanoi; most teachers do not use them very often. Regular taxi's are also available and are cheap compared to Western standards but the cost would soon mount up if that were all you were using.

The most common way to get around is using a motorbike taxi (xe om). They are cheap, convenient and on every other street corner. Foreigners pay about 3,500 dong per kilometer (7,000-10,000 dong would be a typical journey). Haggling is not only acceptable but is expected. I'd recommend that you try and find a xe om driver who speaks a little English to be your regular driver and arrange what days you want to be picked up where.

It may be worthwhile buying your own motorbike, especially if you will be here for more than a year. It will save you a lot of money and your landlord can usually help you find one. It will also give you the freedom to get out of your immediate surroundings. You should still travel by xe om for the first couple of weeks to get an idea of Vietnamese traffic rhythm as it is very unique. It is also highly advisable that you buy health insurance! There is no way that you will be able to register the bike in your name unless you have a residency permit, so will need a local who you trust to have it registered in their name. If it's a powerful motorbike then you'll need a driving license, however you won't need one for a 50cc.

If you have an accident with a non-foreigner you will be to blame, no if's or but's, it's you're fault although technically it is the fault of whoever has the bigger, more powerful vehicle.

Traffic is by far the biggest safety concern. Traffic lights and road signs are definitely not compulsory the question is whether they are to be taken as suggestions or merely ignored! It is getting (slightly) better though, but the roads are definitely more dangerous than those in the first world. Falls from motorbikes are very common but there aren't too many fatalities in the cities, mainly because when accidents occur it is at 15 mph or less. Much more dangerous are the highways in and out of the cities, for instance there are 3-4 casualties per day on the Hanoi highway!

Vietnam Specifics

While it is not as bad as it sounds, and especially for foreigners, it is worth remembering that Vietnam is a communist country and a police state.

Having things posted to Vietnam can be a nightmare. There are no exact regulations, or if there are then the customs officials obviously don't know about them. Generally speaking everything you want to be shipped into Vietnam will be taxed. You are allowed to have "goods" shipped in up to a certain value each month if they are to be used as gifs (I.e. not to sell); the best estimate is 1,000,000 dong a month. A laptop will cost about US$70-150 to clear customs as a gift. Packages will often be opened and arrive months later having been used or damaged and tax is even payable if you have a pair of socks sent to you! It's often actually cheaper to fly to another nearby country and manually bring in items through customs yourself.

Generally speaking if the package was sent within 30 days of your arrival in Vietnam then you shouldn't have to pay taxes. Often packages (especially if sent by the likes of Fed Ex) will face a tax of 50% of the value of the items inside. Postal officials will openly tell you that you should get the sender to lie about the value of the contents. Technically this 50% tax only applies to goods that are already available in Vietnam… technically.

As a foreigner you will be over charged. There is a local rate and a "rich foreigner rate". Some teachers get angry and resentful at this, but if you are willing to learn Vietnamese then you can normally haggle them down substantially.

Bribes and prices depend on how rich you look and how much the Vietnamese think you can afford. It's not uncommon for a bowl of soup that costs US50 cents or less for a local and US$1 for a Western English Teacher to cost a Japanese businessman US$5.

Vietnamese food however is terrible! Some teachers disagree but if you have experienced and enjoyed Vietnamese food in the United States then you are in for a nasty shock. Street food costing US$2 is better than the US50C variety but the supposed problem is that the restaurants here can't get as good quality cooking ingredients as in the western world and often have poor hygiene. If you persevere then you will be bound to find certain restaurants or dishes that are better than average, but lots of teachers relay on the fairly cheap French, Indian, Thai and Japanese restaurants.

As the hygiene isn't great I'd recommend you wipe

your cutlery/chopsticks before eating in restaurants (even the locals do this) and you shouldn't use water out of the tap for drinking. It is generally safe to wash in it, clean your teeth etc.

Some teachers view the Vietnamese as xenophobic. When you consider that before 1975 the only foreigners ever in the country were there with the purpose of blowing large chunks of the country up "for your own good" it's rather more surprising that the Vietnamese are as friendly as they often are or to aspire so much to be like Westerners.

Thailand

Where to Teach

Most teachers initially come to Bangkok and find a job there. Some decide that they want to live in one of the smaller cities and then travel to look for a job in those areas.

You can use Arjan and Dave's Café to find jobs outside of Bangkok and check out to see if the chains have branches if there is somewhere particular you want to teach.

The pay will be less but so should expenses. Outside of Bangkok, your best bets are Hat Yai or Songkhla in the south and Chiang Mai in the north.

Finding Employment

The ideal time to look for work is March- May with the slowest being December-February as often this is when backpackers' money starts running out and they look for teaching jobs to tide them over.

It's best to look for jobs from within the country. Although there is a lot of demand for teachers and some schools do advertise on the internet Thai schools are notorious for not responding to emails. Despite this, once you are in Thailand use the internet to find job listings and especially ***http://www.ajarn.com*** and Dave's Café along with the paper edition of the Bangkok post (the internet version ***http://www.bangkokpost.net/*** omits many of the job adverts). Ajarn is especially good due to the high number of jobs posted each week and has even been credited for teacher's wages increasing in recent years.

Going to schools with a CV is also a good option as long as you arrive looking very presentable. In Bangkok try ECC and the other language schools in Siam Square, Siam Computer at Victory Monument and AUA on Rajadamri Road. These are the head offices of three of the biggest schools that have lots of branches and are all welcoming to applicants who drop in.

Most Asian countries TEFL market is dominated by private language schools. Although there is a large private language school industry here it has been overtaken by the demand for native speakers to teach in state high schools. A few high schools hire directly but most have contracts with private language schools that outsource or agencies to find them teachers If you are employed in a high school then the hours are standard Thai school hours. You will need to be at the school by 7:30am for the flag raising ceremony and finish at 4:30pm. The class sizes at the high schools are normally 40-50 which realistically is too big to see major progress. Thai education has always been good at getting their students to read and write English well but not to speak it. You are hired to help improve their speaking skills as they are exposed to a native speaker. High schools do have cafeterias that the students use and are available for teachers, they are very cheap, the food is good and in some schools the foreign teachers don't even have to pay.

If you are employed directly by a high school then you will generally have to participate in things such as parent-teacher evenings, sports days and the like. You will normally also get 12 weeks paid holiday a year and only teach 15 hours a week although you may have to be onsite longer. If you are working in a high school but employed by a private school then you only have to be onsite when you are teaching but will teach 20-25 hours a week and get no paid holiday.

Private language schools will almost always say that they require you to work a six day week. I would not accept any job that insists on this, and most will reluctantly accept you not working six days a week if you make it clear you will not do so.

Thai work culture is to work whenever you are needed for no overtime and to do everything your boss tells or asks of you. Most Thai managers realize that their foreign teachers will not work like this although there are a few who seem quite confused that westerners are not willing to work on their day off for free. Remember that qualified teachers are in demand in Thailand and don't be afraid to reject unreasonable demands.

Older teachers are not discriminated against at all in Thailand. While, due to short term backpackers, many English language teachers are under 35 Thais would prefer teachers in their late 30's, 40's or 50's as they believe that as you are older you are probably wiser as well.

If you are black then you will find it quite difficult to find a job in Thailand. It is not impossible, especially if you get interviewed by a foreigner rather than a Thai. However lots of recruiters and schools will openly say that they will not even consider a black candidate let alone hire one. Some students admit that they would refuse to be taught by a black teacher and many Thais are even scared of black people because they think they are "evil" or could be criminals!

Pay Rates

Pay in Thailand is relatively low but many consider the lifestyle available here to make up for it.

Finding a job that pays under 30,000baht a month is very easy. Jobs at the 30-40,000 baht level are more competitive but still easily achievable. It is possible to live without western luxuries on 25-30,000 baht but I would feel more comfortable on 35-40,000 baht as a minimum. You can live pretty well but you are definitely not going to save any significant amount of money while working in Thailand, if you save 10,000 baht a month you are doing well.

Private lessons are usually 500-1000 baht an hour.

If you decide to try to negotiate on the pay offered then don't push too hard or they will refuse to offer anything more than they initially did. If you are well presented and joke and have fun with them and it is a Thai interviewing you then you can expect to be able to negotiate 10-25% more than their initial offer.

Tax in Thailand is tricky as every school seems to

charge a different rate depending on how they prefer to conduct tax fraud! Realistically you will be taxed somewhere between 3-10%. Legally it stands at around 6%… probably!

Work Visa

You actually have to have three things to teach legally-a teaching certificate (issued if you have a TEFL cert and BA or an Education degree or a pure English degree), a work permit (based on a letter offering you employment) and a one year visa (based on your work permit).

Before you enter Thailand ask for a non-immigrant B visa. These are increasingly difficult to obtain although they tend to be issued more willingly by consulates than embassies. If you can't get one then you'll need to enter the country on a tourist visa and may have to do a visa run once you've found employment to get one.

You are supposed to get a work permit before you begin teaching but in practice this never happens. The school has to apply for the work permit for you and you are only legally allowed to work for that school, however almost half of English teachers in Thailand don't even have a work visa so the chances of you being caught working illegally is very small.

In addition to this it is likely that most of the private and many of the state school don't realize this restriction! The well connected schools can get you a work visa even if you have no qualifications. Legally you are meant to have a degree and most schools will require you to have one if you want them to apply for a work visa. Once they give you a letter of an offer of employment you need to do a visa run to a neighboring country.

You also need a criminal record check in your country of origin. It is still not clear whether American citizens need a local police check or a FBI check but if Thailand gets its act together and actually decides rather than letting it be up to the mood of any particular official on any random day then my money would be on it being the FBI check.

Check out
www.supersecretpage.com/tefl

4650397